Modern Middle East Nations

AND THEIR STRATEGIC PLACE IN THE WORLD

KUWAIT

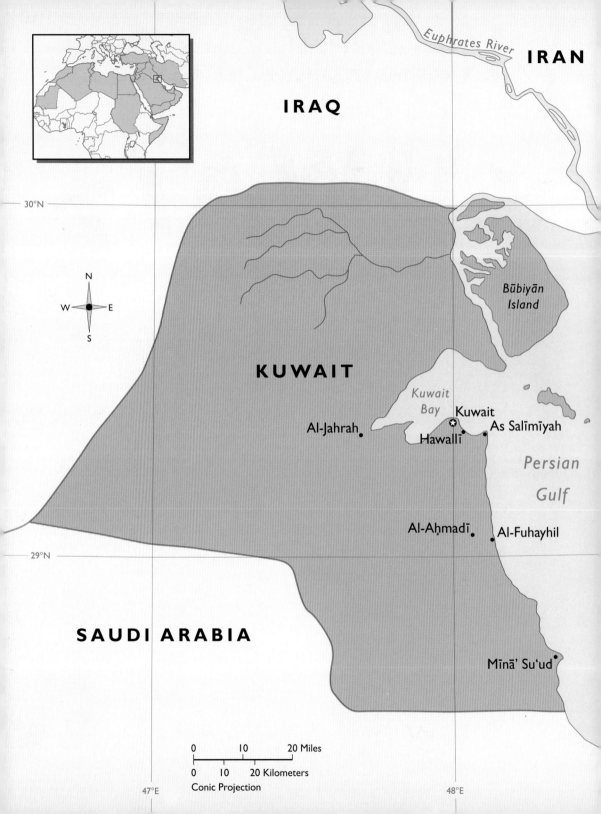

IRAN

Euphrates River

IRAQ

30°N

N
W · E
S

KUWAIT

Būbiyān
Island

Kuwait
Bay

Kuwait

Al-Jahrah

Hawallī

As Salīmīyah

Persian

Gulf

29°N

Al-Aḥmadī

Al-Fuhayhil

SAUDI ARABIA

Mīnā' Suʻud

0   10   20 Miles

0   10   20 Kilometers
Conic Projection

47°E

48°E

Modern Middle East Nations

AND THEIR STRATEGIC PLACE IN THE WORLD

KUWAIT

HAL MARCOVITZ

MASON CREST PUBLISHERS
PHILADELPHIA

Produced by OTTN Publishing, Stockton, New Jersey

Mason Crest Publishers
370 Reed Road
Broomall, PA 19008
www.masoncrest.com

First printing

1 3 5 7 9 8 6 4 2

Library of Congress Cataloging-in-Publication Data

Marcovitz, Hal.
  Kuwait / Hal Marcovitz.
    p. cm. — (Modern Middle East nations and their strategic
place in the world)
Summary: Discusses the geography, history, economy, government,
religion, people, foreign relations, and major cities of Kuwait.
Includes bibliographical references and index.
  ISBN 1-59084-510-2
1. Kuwait—Juvenile literature. [1. Kuwait.] I. Title. II. Series.
DS247.K8M37 2003
953.67—dc21
                                            2002013002

Modern Middle East Nations
AND THEIR STRATEGIC PLACE IN THE WORLD

TABLE OF CONTENTS

Modern Middle East Nations

AND THEIR STRATEGIC PLACE IN THE WORLD

Dr. Harvey Sicherman, president and director of the Foreign Policy Research Institute, is the author of such books as *America the Vulnerable: Our Military Problems and How to Fix Them* (2002) and *Palestinian Autonomy, Self-Government and Peace* (1993).

Introduction

by Dr. Harvey Sicherman

Situated as it is between Africa, Europe, and the Far East, the Middle East has played a unique role in world history. Often described as the birthplace of religions (notably Judaism, Christianity, and Islam) and the cradle of civilizations (Egypt, Mesopotamia, Persia), this region and its peoples have given humanity some of its most precious possessions. At the same time, the Middle East has had more than its share of conflicts. The area is strewn with the ruins of fortifications and the cemeteries of combatants, not to speak of modern arsenals for war.

Today, more than ever, Americans are aware that events in the Middle East can affect our security and prosperity. The United States has a considerable military, political, and economic presence throughout much of the region. Developments there regularly find their way onto the front pages of our newspapers and the screens of our television sets.

Still, it is fair to say that most Middle Eastern countries remain a mystery, their cultures and religions barely known, their peoples and politics confusing and strange. The purpose of this book series is to change that, to educate the reader in the basic facts about the 23 states and many peoples that make up the region. (For our purpose, the Middle East also includes the North African states linked by ethnicity, language, and religion to the Arabs, as well as Somalia and Mauritania, which are African but share the Muslim religion and are members of the Arab League.) A notable feature of the series is the integration of geography, demography, and history; economics and politics; culture and religion. The careful student will learn much that he or she needs to know about ever so important lands.

A few general observations are in order as an introduction to the subject matter.

The first has to do with history and politics. The modern Middle East is full of ancient sites and peoples who trace their lineage and literature to antiquity. Many commentators also attribute the Middle East's political conflicts to grievances and rivalries from the distant past. While history is often invoked, the truth is that the modern Middle East political system dates only from the 1920s and was largely created by the British and the French, the victors of World War I. Such states as Algeria, Iraq, Israel, Jordan, Kuwait, Saudi Arabia, Syria, Turkey, and the United Arab Emirates did not exist before 1914—they became independent between 1920 and 1971. Others, such as Egypt and Iran, were dominated by outside powers until well after World War II. Before 1914, most of the region's states were either controlled by the Turkish-run Ottoman Empire or owed allegiance to the Ottoman sultan. (The sultan was also the caliph or highest religious authority in Islam, in the line of the prophet Muhammad's successors, according to the beliefs of the majority of Muslims known as the Sunni.) It was this imperial Muslim system that was ended by the largely British military victory over the Ottomans in World War I. Few of the leaders who emerged in the wake of this event were happy with the territories they were assigned or the borders, which were often drawn by Europeans. Yet, the system has endured despite many efforts to change it.

The second observation has to do with economics, demography, and natural resources. The Middle Eastern peoples live in a region of often dramatic geographical contrasts: vast parched deserts and high mountains, some with year-round snow; stone-hard volcanic rifts and lush semi-tropical valleys; extremely dry and extremely wet conditions, sometimes separated by only a few miles; large permanent rivers and *wadis*, riverbeds dry as a bone until winter rains send torrents of flood from the mountains to the sea. In ancient times, a very skilled agriculture made the Middle East the breadbasket of the Roman Empire, and its trade carried luxury fabrics, foods, and spices both East and West.

Most recently, however, the Middle East has become more known for a single commodity—oil, which is unevenly distributed and largely concentrated in the Persian Gulf and Arabian Peninsula (although large pockets are also to be found in Algeria, Libya, and other sites). There are also new, potentially lucrative offshore gas fields in the Eastern Mediterranean.

This uneven distribution of wealth has been compounded by demographics. Birth rates are very high, but the countries with the most oil are often lightly populated. Over the last decade, Middle East populations under the age of 20 have grown enormously. How will these young people be educated? Where will they work? The failure of most governments in the region to give their people skills and jobs (with notable exceptions such as Israel) has also contributed to large out-migrations. Many have gone to Europe; many others work in other Middle Eastern countries, supporting their families from afar.

Another unsettling situation is the heavy pressure both people and industry have put on vital resources. Chronic water shortages plague the region. Air quality, public sanitation, and health services in the big cities are also seriously overburdened. There are solutions to these problems, but they require a cooperative approach that is sorely lacking.

A third important observation is the role of religion in the Middle East. Americans, who take separation of church and state for granted, should know that most countries in the region either proclaim their countries to be Muslim or allow a very large role for that religion in public life. Among those with predominantly Muslim populations, Turkey alone describes itself as secular and prohibits avowedly religious parties in the political system. Lebanon was a Christian-dominated state, and Israel continues to be a Jewish state. While both strongly emphasize secular politics, religion plays an enormous role in culture, daily life, and legislation. It is also important to recall that Islamic law (*Sharia*) permits people to prac-tice Judaism and Christianity in Muslim states but only as *Dhimmi*, protected but very second-class citizens.

Fourth, the American student of the modern Middle East will be impressed by the varieties of one-man, centralized rule, very unlike the workings of Western democracies. There are monarchies, some with traditional methods of consultation for tribal elders and even ordinary citizens, in Saudi Arabia and many Gulf States; kings with limited but still important parliaments (such as in Jordan and

Morocco); and military and civilian dictatorships, some (such as Syria) even operating on the hereditary principle (Hafez al Assad's son Bashar succeeded him). Turkey is a practicing democracy, although a special role is given to the military that limits what any government can do. Israel operates the freest democracy, albeit constricted by emergency regulations (such as military censorship) due to the Arab-Israeli conflict.

In conclusion, the MODERN MIDDLE EAST NATIONS series will engage imagination and interest simply because it covers an area of such great importance to the United States. Americans may be relative latecomers to the affairs of this region, but our involvement there will endure. We at the Foreign Policy Research Institute hope that these books will kindle a lifelong interest in the fascinating and significant Middle East.

One of Kuwait's most famous man-made landmarks is Kuwait Towers, located in the capital city near the waterfront. The tallest tower is nearly 600 feet (180 meters) tall; the tower on the left supports a large water tank. Both were damaged during the Iraqi occupation, although the damage is not visible from the outside.

Place in the World

When firefighters from Texas arrived in Kuwait in the spring of 1991, they did not find the sandy deserts described in the tales of Scheherazade, the 10th-century princess who told the exotic and magical stories in *A Thousand and One Arabian Nights*. Nor did they find a prosperous community of privileged and wealthy **sheiks** made rich by the seemingly bottomless stores of oil beneath their feet. No, the Kuwait the Texans found off the shores of the Persian Gulf was a country torn by war, looted by its invaders, and on the verge of becoming the center of a world-wide ecological catastrophe.

Just a few days after Iraqi troops were driven out of Kuwait by a **coalition** of armies led by the United States, firefighters from the United States and Canada were called in to extinguish oil field infernos that had been ignited by the invaders. Before fleeing the country, the troops under Iraqi dictator Saddam Hussein had set fire to 647 oil wells in Kuwait, sending bright orange, red, and yellow flames high into the cloudless desert sky. Each day, an estimated five million barrels of crude oil—worth some $87 million—burned from the wells. Fighting the fires was dangerous; the firefighters in the Kuwait desert, found themselves facing flames burning as hot as 4,000° Fahrenheit (2,200° Celsius). But more significantly, the dense smoke and soot from the fires blackened the sky over the tiny country, turning day into night. The environmental impact could be felt as far as 1,600 miles (2,575 km) away—in the state of Kashmir, India, people saw a black-tinged snowfall.

Saddam's troops had occupied Kuwait for seven months. The Iraqi dictator sent his soldiers across the border on August 2, 1990, declaring Kuwait the 19th province of Iraq, a much larger country with a formidable, battle-hardened army. Saddam chose to invade Kuwait because the *emirate* is one of the keystones of the world's oil supply. Indeed, tiny Kuwait sits atop what is believed to be 10 percent of the world's oil reserves. Although Iraq and Kuwait are both members of the Organization of *Petroleum* Exporting Countries (OPEC)—the 11-nation *cartel* that controls much of the world's oil—Kuwait often decided on its own whether to increase or decrease oil production, which in turn affected the price of the *commodity* across the world. In the months preceding the Iraqi invasion, Kuwait had stepped up oil production, which drove down the price of crude. Saddam was desperate for money; his nation had recently concluded a long and expensive war against neighboring Iran. With oil prices low and Saddam insisting on retaining a huge military force, Iraq faced bankruptcy.

Kuwait has often found itself caught up in the twisted world of Middle East politics for reasons other than its decisions regarding the oil market. Kuwaiti rulers have opposed the spread of Islamic fundamentalism—the radical movement among *Muslims* who

Ceremonial dancers celebrate as the last oil fire in Kuwait is extinguished, November 6, 1991. Since the end of the Gulf War, Kuwait has spent more than $160 billion rebuilding the country.

believe in a strict interpretation of the Islamic holy book known as the **Qur'an** (or Koran). In 1979, Shi'a fundamentalists under the Ayatollah Khomeini led a revolution in nearby Iran that toppled Shah Muhammad Reza Pahlavi from power. Since then, Arab leaders have feared similar uprisings in their countries—particularly in the Islamic nations ruled by royal families, such as Kuwait. By the 1990s the **Islamist** movement had spread to other countries, most notably Afghanistan, where the fundamentalist Taliban government allowed terrorist leader Osama bin Laden to run training camps in the country. Terrorists trained in those camps led the suicide attacks on the World Trade Center and Pentagon on September 11, 2001, that caused the deaths of more than 3,000 Americans and prompted an invasion of Afghanistan by U.S. troops.

Kuwait is one of the few Arab states to offer its people some form of political participation. The country has a constitution that assures its citizens some freedoms, although the **emir** has a great amount of authority. Since 1962, Kuwait's emirs have given their people a limited role in the operation of the government by permitting the election of lawmakers to a **parliament**. In recent years,

Kuwaiti women have agitated for the right to vote—a rare privilege for women in most Arabic countries, where Islamic law that limits women's rights is strictly observed. Measures granting women the right to vote have been narrowly defeated in Kuwait's parliament.

Kuwait finds itself constantly pushed and pulled by Arab sentiments toward the West. Though representatives of the anti-American fundamentalist movement have gained seats in

Environmental Catastrophe

After the 1991 Gulf War ended, it took nine months for American and Canadian firefighters to extinguish all the oil field fires. During that time, leaves on trees throughout the Persian Gulf states became coated with a thin film of oil. In the gulf itself, the tiny oil droplets hit the saltwater surface and were absorbed by plankton, which was ingested by the fish life in the gulf. Thus, the Iraqi vandalism of the wells in Kuwait briefly wiped out a source of food for many countries. Very old and very young Kuwaitis suffered from breathing ailments caused by the thick smoke. Kuwait has virtually no agricultural production, but in nearby countries where fruits, grains, and vegetables are raised the oil droplets turned the soil acidic, destroying thousands of acres of crops.

Another environmental impact of the Gulf War grew out of the creation of oil lakes by the Iraqi troops. While most of the oil gushing out of the derricks during the fires ignited and burned off, some 30,000 barrels a day spilled directly onto Kuwait soil, pooling in depressed areas and forming black lakes of crude. Often, the lakes themselves would catch fire, sending clouds of dense smoke and fumes into the atmosphere. The lakes also trapped birds and other wildlife, usually killing the animals. Another danger posed by the lakes is that many of them are believed to cover explosive mines buried by the Iraqis. The government in Kuwait has been cleaning up the oil lakes since the end of the Gulf War.

Iraqi soldiers created still more mayhem when they dug channels into the desert near the coast and filled the channels with crude oil. The channels were then set ablaze. The channels were dug under the notion that they could serve as a first line of defense in the event of an invasion.

U.S. Secretary of Defense Donald H. Rumsfeld is greeted by American soldiers stationed at Camp Doha, a 500-acre complex near Kuwait City. The United States has maintained a military presence in Kuwait since the end of the Gulf War. In the fall of 2002, there were several shooting attacks in Kuwait in which U.S. soldiers were killed or injured. In at least one fatal attack, the Kuwaiti gunmen had links to Osama bin Laden's al-Qaeda terrorist network.

parliament, the emir, Sheik Jabir al-Sabah, has asked the United States to maintain a military presence in Kuwait because he still fears Iraqi aggression. The United States has responded by stationing some 5,000 troops in the country. On the streets of Kuwait City, though, many young citizens view terrorist leaders like bin Laden as freedom fighters for standing up against the West. They have denounced the United States for its support of Israel.

In the years since the Iraqi invasion, Kuwait has become a place of stability in a turbulent Middle East that is often torn by conflict, changing allegiances, and obscure beliefs that can easily be misunderstood by westerners. The lives and livelihoods of many Americans are directly affected by decisions made by the people of Kuwait and their leaders.

An artificial island lies offshore from Kuwait City. With the money received from its oil, the people of Kuwait have attempted to modify their harsh desert environment to make it a more pleasant place to live.

The Land

T he swashbuckling British soldier T. E. Lawrence, who helped lead an Arab revolt in 1916, spent months crossing the Arabian Peninsula on the back of a camel. While leading the Arab uprising against the **Ottoman** Turks, Lawrence came to admire the desert people, in no small part because of their ability to survive in one of the most inhospitable climates on earth. "These inhabited hills and plains framed a gulf of thirsty desert," Lawrence wrote.

Kuwait is one of the nations located on the Arabian Peninsula. It can be found on the peninsula's eastern shore along the Persian Gulf. The country is hardly what anyone could consider a lazy seaside resort. The Arabian Desert reaches practically to the waters of the gulf, making virtually the entire landscape unsuitable for agriculture.

Lawrence found the deserts of Kuwait sandy, although he described regions where the sand took on the consistency of gravel, "making the road difficult." Of course, in Lawrence's day men traveled on the backs of horses and camels. Decades later, the coarse reddish-brown sands of the Kuwaiti desert provided few obstacles to the Bradley fighting vehicles and M-1 Abrams tanks deployed by the U.S. Army during the Persian Gulf War.

During the intensely hot and dry summers, daytime temperatures in Kuwait average between 108° and 115°F (42° to 46° C), although it is not unusual for the thermometer to spike up to 125°F (41°C). The hottest months of the year fall between May and October. In August and September, the winds bring in sea air from the Persian Gulf, which increases the humidity.

Kuwait is located just 300 miles (483 kilometers) north of the Tropic of Cancer, and that has a lot to do with why the heat is so oppressive. The regions on Earth that receive the most direct sunlight fall between or near the lines of latitude known as the tropics of Cancer, in the northern hemisphere, and Capricorn, in the southern hemisphere. The tropics lie 23-1/2 degrees above and below the equator. This region is known as the **_Torrid Zone_**. Lands bordering the Torrid Zone feature climates that are no less inhospitable than countries within the zone.

There is more than just direct sunlight affecting the desert climate. Gigantic air swirls are created by the revolution of the earth. These air swirls lose heat as they reach the upper atmosphere, then rise in temperature again as they descend on the Torrid Zone. This constant barrage of sunlight and hot air has dried out the soil, making it incapable of trapping any moisture that might fall as rain. As a result, rainfall in Kuwait averages between just 3 and 6 inches (8 and 15 centimeters) a year.

Since the soil can't hold water, virtually nothing can grow in the desert. Just 1 percent of Kuwaiti territory is farmland. The main crops are olives and dates—hardy fruits that are capable of withstanding Kuwait's inhospitable climate. In recent years, Kuwaiti

Much of Kuwait is low-lying desert, as this map shows. Oil fields can be found throughout the country. Kuwait has a large reserve of oil; major oil fields include the Raudhatian and Sabriyah fields in the north, the Magwa, Ahmadi, Burgan, and Minagish fields in the southeast-central part of the country, and the Umm Gudair and al-Wafra fields in the south. It is estimated that Kuwait controls about 10 percent of the world's oil reserves.

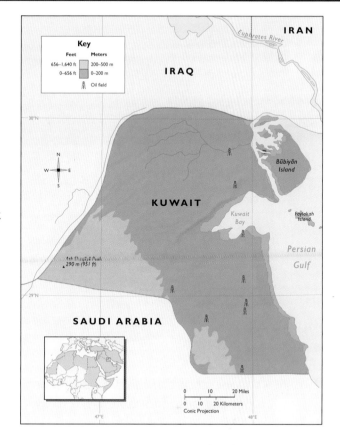

farmers have used irrigation to help them grow tomatoes and cucumbers.

Many of the country's farms are located in al-Wafra, an irrigated desert region near Kuwait's southern border. In al-Wafra, the government is developing a complex of agricultural laboratories, reservoirs, and greenhouses.

Even Kuwait's winters are relatively warm. In January, daytime temperatures average between 50° and 80°F (10° and 27°C). At night, 40°F (4°C) is about as cold as it will get. Rarely does the temperature drop below freezing.

Most Kuwaitis escape the desert heat by living in homes that are air-conditioned—a luxury few of them could afford before the discovery of oil. Prior to the oil boom years, Kuwaitis cooled their homes by erecting wind towers on top of their roofs. The towers

Two views of the desert in Kuwait. The country's location in the Torrid Zone makes it a hot and uncomfortable place to live.

contained large hollow shafts, the center part of which was divided into four equal V-shaped sections designed to catch the wind and direct it down into the home.

Their oil wealth has enabled Kuwaitis to employ unusual and expensive methods to beat the heat. In the 1960s, as Kuwait was first coming to terms with its vast wealth, government leaders considered a plan to enclose the entire nation under an air-conditioned dome. In recent years, some more practical methods have been employed. For example, Kuwaitis have embraced winter sports—the country's capital, Kuwait City, contains the first two ice skating rinks constructed in the Middle East. One of the rinks is Olympic-sized and serves as the home of the Kuwait Falcons, the city's ice hockey team. Surrounding the rink are seats to accommodate 1,600 fans. Instructors from Sweden have emigrated to Kuwait to teach the local residents how to skate.

NATURAL FEATURES AND WILDLIFE

There are no freshwater rivers or lakes in Kuwait, and no wells that produce water for drinking. Water found in Kuwait's wells is brackish, meaning it contains salt that has seeped beneath the soil from the nearby Persian Gulf. **Desalinization** plants that remove salt from seawater provide Kuwait with fresh water by processing water pumped out of the gulf.

There is no range of mountains offering a grand backdrop to Kuwait's horizontal, featureless landscape. The country is flat, sloping just slightly from the interior toward the gulf. One of the few recognizable features of the Kuwait landscape is the rocky al-Mutla ridge just northwest of Kuwait City, where allied aircraft swept down on retreating Iraqi forces during the closing days of the Gulf War. Another ridge of hills stretches across the country, running from the northeast to the southwest. These hills are composed of limestone and sand dunes. One hill, known as Jal AzZor, overlooks the coast of Kuwait Bay. During the times of Kuwait's brief rainfalls, water runs off the hills into valleys where desert grass and wildflowers grow, providing pastureland for sheep and camels. For the most part, though, there is little native plant life in Kuwait.

As for animal life, the desert is by no means teeming with critters. However, if a visitor knows where to look it is possible to catch a glimpse of mammals, lizards, and birds as well as unusual spiders and insects. At the occasional desert oasis, tiny animals such as gerbils, rabbits, rats, mice, foxes, and hedgehogs are able to find enough to eat. They often fall prey to jackals, fierce wolf-like animals that hunt and howl at night.

A desert lizard known as the dhub makes its home in burrows

The Geography of Kuwait

Location: Middle East, bordering the Persian Gulf, between Iraq and Saudi Arabia

Area: slightly smaller than New Jersey
    total: 6,880 square miles (17,820 sq km)
    land: 6,880 square miles (17,820 sq km)
    water: 0 square miles (0 sq km)

Borders: Iraq, 149 miles (240 km); Saudi Arabia, 138 miles (222 km); coastline 310 miles (499 km)

Climate: dry desert; intensely hot summers; short, cool winters

Terrain: flat to slightly undulating desert plain

Elevation extremes:
    lowest point: Persian Gulf 0 feet (0 meters)
    highest point: Ash-Shaqaya, 951 feet (290 meters)

Natural hazards: sudden cloudbursts are common from October to April; they bring heavy rain which can damage roads and houses; sandstorms and dust storms occur throughout the year, but are most common between March and August

Source: Adapted from CIA World Factbook, 2002.

Camels graze on tiny plants in the Kuwaiti desert. Arab traders domesticated camels thousands of years ago to help them travel through the desert.

dug into the sandy Kuwait landscape. The dhub will expand its chest and hiss menacingly at predators, including humans. For centuries, **Bedouin** tribesmen have hunted dhubs for food.

Dhubs must also be wary of another natural enemy, the sand boa snake. The sand boa is nonpoisonous, but kills by wrapping its body around its prey and squeezing it to death. There are many other snakes found in Kuwait, including the poisonous Arabian rear-fanged snake, whose fangs are located in the back of its mouth. Another deadly snake found in the Kuwait desert is the black cobra, which is rarely seen. Many Bedouins believe that if they kill a black cobra they will be haunted by the snake's spirit.

Camels are, of course, a frequent sight in Kuwait. Even in the age of the all-terrain vehicle, camel herds led by Bedouins can be seen crossing the desert. Bedouin herdsmen also raise sheep and goats.

The desert air and soil are alive with many varieties of insects and spiders. Sand flies, black flies, mosquitoes, cockroaches, lice, ticks, and centipedes can be found in the country. Kuwaitis often see a long-legged black beetle that has adapted very well to the harsh conditions—it is one of the few insects that can be seen in the sun during the hottest part of the day. One common and pesky insect is the camel fly, which is aggressive and capable of delivering a painful bite.

Kuwaitis must be wary of spiders. Poisonous scorpions are abundant in the desert. American soldiers serving in Kuwait have been warned against wearing sandals, jogging in the desert, and putting on their boots before checking inside to see if unfriendly arachnids have made a home inside their footwear.

Long before oil was discovered in the country, many Kuwaitis made their livings in the fishing and pearling industries. While the development of cultured pearls has destroyed the Gulf pearl industry, the waters off the coast of the country are home to abundant marine life, and there is still a fishing industry based in Kuwait. Small Kuwaiti boats, as well as vessels from nearby countries, find shrimp in abundant numbers off the coast. Gilled fish caught off the shores of Kuwait include shad, grunt, mullet, grouper, sea bream, snapper, and croaker.

In September 2001, some 2,000 tons of dead fish washed ashore along the Kuwait coastline. Investigators said an abundance of streptococcus bacteria in the waters near Kuwait caused the deaths. In humans, streptococcus can cause numerous illnesses, including scarlet fever and tonsillitis. During the crisis, government officials in Kuwait banned the sale of fresh fish in the country's markets, fearing the infected fish could spread diseases. It was several weeks before fishermen were able to return to Kuwait's coast.

More than 300 species of birds can be found living in Kuwait, but just 16 species are native breeders, meaning they nest in Kuwait year-round. The most common native breeders include species of doves, sparrows, pigeons, mynahs, and nightingales. The others are migratory species that fly in from nearby countries, mostly following the shoreline along the Persian Gulf. They include hummingbirds, larks, robins, kingfishers, bluethroats, martins,

A fisherman displays his catch at a seaside fish market. Historically, Kuwait has had a strong fishing industry; fishing remains an important occupation in the country today.

swallows, and warblers. The muddy areas near the coast provide nesting areas for herons, egrets, gulls, and terns. Flamingos, owls, and parakeets also visit, but are not believed to breed in Kuwait. Following the Gulf War, when the air was choked by smoke and the vegetation and beach sands were coated with an oily film, most birds stayed away. In the years following the war, however, the bird populations have returned.

Again, what won't grow or live in the desert can be obtained if the money is available. Many Kuwaitis maintain green lawns around their homes by importing grass, soil, and fertilizer from other countries. Also, the government has established a world-class zoo in Kuwait that features hundreds of exotic animals.

DISPUTED BORDERS

The tiny nation of Kuwait covers just 6,880 square miles (17,820 square kilometers). It is roughly the size of New Jersey. The triangular-shaped country can be found at the northeastern corner of the Arabian Peninsula. It is bordered to the north and northwest by Iraq and to the southwest by Saudi Arabia. About 310 miles (499

Iraqi vehicles submerged in a lake of oil after the 1990–91 occupation. The Gulf War and its aftermath was an environmental disaster in Kuwait. In addition to the noxious smoke from oil fires, large areas of desert sand were covered with sticky black oil that had been vented by Iraqi troops.

km) of Kuwait's coastline faces the gulf. At its most distant points, Kuwait is about 125 miles (201 km) north to south and 106 miles (171 km) east to west.

The lowest point in the country is its coastline with the Persian Gulf, which is at sea level. The highest point in the country is in the southwest, where the sand rises at one point to about 951 feet (290 meters) above sea level—less than half the average elevation found in the United States.

There is more to Kuwait's weather than just hot and sunny days. Although it rains little in Kuwait, cloudbursts from October to April can occur at any time. Of much more concern are dust storms, known in Kuwait as the *shammal*, which can occur any time during the year but are most common from March to August. Getting caught in a *shammal* with its heavy winds and blinding sand gusts could be fatal.

Over the years the Kuwaitis have never enjoyed undisputed borders with either the Saudis or the Iraqis. Along Kuwait's border with Saudi Arabia lies a 2,200 square mile (5,700 sq km) area known as the "Neutral Zone." Both countries claim ownership of the zone. The zone includes little more than desert; however, the land contains valuable oil reserves. Both countries have agreed to share equally the oil produced in the Neutral Zone.

Kuwait's border dispute with Iraq is much more fractious, and was partly responsible for the Iraqi invasion in 1990. Over the years, many Iraqi leaders have refused to recognize their country's borders with Kuwait, arguing that Kuwaiti territory was awarded to Iraq in the treaties following the collapse of the Ottoman Empire and the end of World War I. Still others in Iraq believed that while Kuwait may be **autonomous**, their country could claim ownership at least to the islands of Bubiyan and Warbah. Following the Gulf War the United Nations established a commission to clearly define Kuwait's border with Iraq. The commission ruled the true border was actually about 1,870 feet (570 meters) further north than it had been before the war, which placed the Iraqi oil field at Ar Rumaylah into Kuwaiti territory. The new border also awarded Kuwait partial ownership of the Iraqi military base at Umm Qasr.

ISLANDS OF KUWAIT

A number of islands in the Persian Gulf are claimed by Kuwait. The larger islands include Bubiyan, Warbah, and Failaka. The islands are sparsely populated but are valuable to the Kuwaitis because of their oil reserves.

Failaka lies about 12.5 miles (20.1 km) across Kuwait Bay directly east of Kuwait City. It covers about 9.3 square miles (24 sq km) and for many years supported a population of people working in the fishing and pearling trades. In addition, the land is fertile, so farmers have made their homes on Failaka since the Bronze Age. One of the antiquities on Failaka left behind by early Greek residents is a 12-room house containing a blacksmith shop and tile workshop. One of the tiles found in the workshop bore the image of Alexander the Great, who spread Greek culture throughout the region during his conquests in the fourth century B.C. Archaeologists have also unearthed an old fortress that includes remnants of a stone pillar, statues of Greek gods, and a limestone plaque indicating the fortress was also used as a cultural center.

The island also has considerable oil resources, and petroleum extraction and processing is now the primary occupation of people who travel to work on Failaka. In 1990, Failaka was captured by Iraqi soldiers, forcing the inhabitants to flee their homes. Most have never returned, and today the Kuwaiti military has established a base on the island. In October 2002 a U.S. Marine was shot and killed on the island in an attack by suspected members of the al-Qaeda terrorist group.

Two smaller islands are located near Failaka. They include Miskan and Auhah islands. Miskan is less than a mile (1.6 km) long and just 2,600 feet (793 meters) wide. Miskan contains a lighthouse. Auhah is long and skinny—it measures about 10 miles (16 km) from end to end and about 2,500 feet (763 meters) across. Fish are plentiful around the island, but because Auhah is located in shallow waters only small craft dare anchor near the island.

To the south, off the coast of the Kuwait-Saudi Arabia border, lies Umm al-Maradim Island. Umm al-Maradim is located in deep water, which enables ships to anchor along its coast. The island is just about a mile (1.6 km) long and less than 2,000 feet (610 meters) wide. It is one of the few places in Kuwaiti waters where divers still seek pearls. Many birds flock to Umm al-Maradim, and during times of rain green vegetation grows in abundance.

A small island near Umm al-Maradim is Garuh, which is not much more than a sand patch measuring about 300 yards (275 meters) by 200 yards (183 meters). There is a 45 foot (14 meter) tower on the island to help ships navigate, as well as a radio station and police outpost. From above, a coral reef can be seen surrounding the island.

Another island that attracts birds is Kubbar, which is about 12 miles (19 km) east of the Kuwait coastal city of al-Fuhayhil. So many gulls flock to the island

For centuries boats that obtained fresh water from the Shatt al-Arab, a river that separates Iran and Iraq, supplied Kuwait's drinking water. In 1953, the country established its first of two desalinization plants, which remove salt from seawater through a distillation process. Together, the two plants process some 138 million gallons of water a day.

that Kuwaiti officials have designated Kubbar a bird sanctuary. Flamingoes can also be found nesting on Kubbar. Currently, Kubbar contains a solar-powered lighthouse and landing pad for helicopters. Eventually, Kuwaiti officials hope to develop facilities on Kubbar where tourists can view the birds without disturbing their habitats.

The largest of Kuwait's islands is Bubiyan, which measures some 263 square miles (681 sq km). Located across a narrow channel from Bubiyan is Warbah Island, which covers about 14 square miles (36 sq km).

Bubiyan and Warbah are strategically important to Kuwait's security because they form a natural barrier between the country and the border regions of Iran and Iraq. The government believes both islands contain significant oil reserves. The government has erected a bridge connecting Bubiyan and the mainland.

This Arabic manuscript illustration, created in the mid-16th century, shows Muhammad riding to heaven with an escort of angels. In the 7th century A.D. Muhammad's teachings became the basis for a new religion, Islam, which soon swept throughout the Arabian Peninsula.

History

Saddam Hussein was not the first Iraqi dictator to plan a conquest of Kuwait. In 1961, the Iraqi leader Abd al-Karim Qasim moved troops to the Kuwait border and threatened an invasion. Kuwaitis had much to fear from Qasim. Three years earlier, Qasim had seized power in Iraq by murdering the royal family. Qasim called off the invasion when Great Britain rushed troops to Kuwait and vowed to protect the tiny emirate.

With much anxiety, the Kuwaitis have watched unsteady and strong-arm regimes come to power in other Middle East countries. During the 1950s, Kuwaitis feared the intentions of Egyptian President Gamal Abdel Nasser, who envisioned a unified Arab empire—led by Egypt, of course. Nasser posed a threat because he had supported revolutions in other Arab countries, such as Yemen. During the 1980s, Kuwaitis worried that a fundamentalist Islamic uprising would be sparked in their country by the followers of Ayatollah Khomeini in Iran. Other Middle East countries have posed threats as well.

Except for the invasion launched by Saddam in 1990, the Kuwaitis have usually managed to find their way out of trouble through the use of diplomacy, negotiation, and—as the country found itself awash in oil—money. After the British forced Qasim to back down in 1961, Kuwaiti leaders agreed to invest $84 million in Iraq. Earlier, the Kuwaitis had managed to keep Nasser at bay by providing $140 million in assistance to his country.

Throughout the 250-year history of Kuwait, the nation has been led by just one family—the al-Sabah. Over time, members of the family have earned a reputation as shrewd negotiators. They gained control of the country by striking a deal with two rival families who agreed to let the al-Sabah rule the desert kingdom because they saw little potential in the inhospitable wasteland. Of course, in 1752 no one envisioned the riches that lay beneath the sands.

Bedouins had been making their way through the area long before the al-Sabahs arrived. The first visitors to Kuwait who left

An Iraqi cavalry unit on parade in Baghdad, 1960. In June 1961 Iraqi dictator Abd al-Karim Qasim prepared his military to attack Kuwait, which it claimed as Iraqi territory. Intervention by Great Britain protected Kuwait.

By the time of his death Alexander the Great (356–323 B.C.) ruled an empire that included much of Asia, the Middle East, and eastern Europe. His conquests spread Greek culture throughout the region. Although Alexander died before invading the Arabian Peninsula, Greek settlers eventually established a colony on Failaka Island, part of modern-day Kuwait.

behinds remnants of their civilization were the Dilmun, a Bronze Age sailing and trading people from Bahrain who established a settlement on Failaka Island between 2300 B.C. and 1100 B.C. In 325 B.C. the Macedonian conqueror Alexander the Great planned an invasion of the Arabian Peninsula. Alexander died before the invasion commenced, however, and the Greeks never conquered the region. Though Greeks established a colony on Failaka, which they named Ikaros, by 250 B.C. Greek influence in the region had been replaced by the Parthians, a Persian dynasty that controlled much of the Middle East.

ARRIVAL OF THE PROPHET

For the next eight centuries, not much was happening in the northeastern corner of the Arabian Peninsula. The land was so inhospitable that no one but hardy nomads could endure the unforgiving desert sun. In other parts of the peninsula, though, important changes were occurring. In about the year A.D. 570, the **Prophet** Muhammad was born.

At first, Muhammad led a normal and quite unremarkable life in the Arabian city of Mecca, about 800 miles (129 km) southwest of Kuwait. He was a member of the Hashem clan. In later years, members of that clan would go on to rule several Arab countries. (Today, the lone Hashemite ruler still in power is King Abdullah II of Jordan.)

When he was 40, Muhammad started having visions in which he was told, "Recite! You are the Messenger of God!" God (known to Muslims as Allah) then commanded Muhammad to repeat His words, which came to be known as the Qur'an—the holy book of **Islam**. It took several years for Muhammad to recite the laws; when he spoke, his words were copied down on scraps of leather, flat stone tablets, and even camel bones by his followers. (Muhammad himself was unable to read or write.)

In English, Islam means "submission to God." To accept Islam is to accept five basic laws: *shahada*—the tenet that there is one god, Allah, and that Muhammad was his messenger; *salat*—the duty to pray five times a day; *sawm*—the observance of Ramadan, the holy month in which it is necessary to fast from sunup to sundown; *zakat*—the tradition of donating to charity; and *hajj*—the obligation of all Muslims to make a pilgrimage to Mecca, the holy city, at least once in their lifetime.

At first, Arabs in Mecca and elsewhere refused to accept the new religion. Many of them worshiped multiple deities and they rejected the idea of one god. Slowly, the Arab people began converting. Most of the early followers were drawn to Islam by the personal appeal of Muhammad, a persuasive and charismatic leader who seemed to possess a gift for resolving disputes. Others joined Islam after Muslim armies conquered them. Unlike the first Christians, who had been taught to turn the other cheek, the Muslims were prepared to fight to spread the word of the prophet. The religion soon spread throughout the Middle East, northern Africa, and even into

This Kuwaiti sailing dhow, *al-Muhallab*, was the last surviving from Kuwait's age of sail. Many Kuwaitis made their living from the sea before oil was discovered in the 1930s. The ship was destroyed during Iraq's 1990–91 occupation of Kuwait.

parts of Europe and Asia.

Although the rise of Islam was an important development that transformed the Arab world, the region that is now Kuwait would remain unsettled desert territory for another millennium.

THE ROOTS OF PRESENT-DAY KUWAIT

During the early 1700s a tribe of Arabs known as the Bani Utubs settled along the coast of the Persian Gulf in the region that is now known as Kuwait. The Bani Utubs had been living in central Arabia, but made their way to the coast after a period of drought and famine. Their main settlement was located along the southern shore of a natural bay, where Kuwait City stands today. The sandy desert to the west of the gulf was as inhospitable as the barren land the Bani Utubs had left in central Arabia, but the bay provided a natural harbor for fishing boats as well as pearlers.

Although the Bani Utubs were probably the first settlers, the region was not unknown. Dutch mapmakers had charted the terri-

A 17th-century Mamluk dagger, encrusted with rubies, on display at the Kuwait National Museum. The Mamluks controlled the Kuwait region by the early 13th century, eventually taking control of much of the Middle East. Mamluk power was centered in Cairo, Egypt.

tory, labeling the region with the name "Grane." The word was derived from the Arabic term *qurain*, which means "hill."

The tribe was composed of three main families: the al-Sabahs, al-Khalifas, and al-Jalahimas. The three families decided to split up authority over the settlement among themselves. The al-Khalifas would be responsible for the pearl trade while the al-Jalahimas took control of fishing. The al-Sabahs agreed to become administrators of the settlement. At the time, the al-Khalifas and al-Jalahimas probably thought they got the better end of the deal, as at this time the village was composed of little more than tents. Still, the al-Sabahs took control of the village, and around 1756 Sabah bin Jabir bin Adhbi became the first emir, or prince, of the settlement. This marked the real beginning of the country known as Kuwait. Any one of the three families could have declared itself outright ruler and then fought the other two, but the settlers saw no reason to resort to bloodshed when negotiation would work just as well. That philosophy has dominated Kuwaiti thinking into the 21st century. Eventually, both the al-Jalahimas and al-Khalifas left the village.

In 1760, the al-Sabahs, seeking protection from other Arab tribes, erected a wall made of dried mud around the settlement. The wall gave the settlement the appearance of a fort. In Arabic, the word "Kuwait" translates roughly to "Little Fort."

> After leaving Kuwait in the 18th century, the al-Khalifas settled first in Qatar and then Bahrain, where they established a monarchy. The family continues to rule Bahrain today.

The fort would prove to be largely unnecessary. The al-Sabahs preferred negotiation to combat, and managed to live in peace for centuries with their stronger neighbors. Across the gulf, Persia cared little about the tiny emirate and was more concerned with protecting itself against larger and more dangerous enemies. Over the centuries, the al-Sabahs were able to negotiate treaties with the tribes that roamed the Arabian peninsula.

At this time the Ottoman Turks controlled much of the Middle East. This powerful empire, based in Turkey, had conquered most of the populated areas of the peninsula during the 15th century. However, the Ottomans seemed to have little interest in this dusty emirate until the 1890s, when the Turks eyed Kuwait as the terminus of a grand railroad project they planned with the Germans that would link the Persian Gulf to Berlin.

The Kuwaitis turned to Great Britain for protection from Ottoman rule. For their part, the British were more than eager to aid the emirate and gain a foothold in the Persian Gulf. The British Navy had been patrolling the gulf for much of the 1800s to protect India, which at the time was a colony of Great Britain.

As far back as 1841, the British had considered the benefits of enlisting Kuwait as an ally. Here is how Captain S. Hennell, a British diplomat, summed up Kuwait in a letter to his superiors:

> Its harbour is certainly an exceedingly fine one, capable of holding the navy of Great Britain, but so far as my observation goes, it possesses no other advantage. The country around is a salt and sandy desert, of the most barren and inhospitable description, with not a tree or shrub visible, as far as the eye can reach, excepting a few bushes which mark the wells. From the taste and quality of the water, I feel almost certain that it would not agree with the constitutions of either Europeans or Indians.

Hennell went on to say that the citizens of Kuwait City showed a surprising prosperity for desert dwellers, for there seemed to be little feuding and factionalism, which "render them respected and feared by all other Maritime Tribes."

In 1892, Britain offered to establish a military base in Kuwait. The Kuwaiti ruler, Muhammad, refused the offer, fearing that such a bold move would provoke a war with the Ottomans. His half-brother Mubarek opposed Muhammad, arguing that the Ottomans intended to **annex** Kuwait. In 1896, Mubarek assassinated Muhammad. This bloody **coup** marks the only time in Kuwait's history that power within the al-Sabah family changed hands violently. Mubarek feared that in return he would be deposed in an Ottoman-backed coup, so he invited the British to establish their base. In 1899, Mubarek signed a treaty giving Great Britain control over Kuwait's foreign policy. This meant that the Turks could not extend their railway into Kuwait without British permission. The British, anxious to keep their European rival Germany out of the region, were not likely to give that permission. The Turks still claimed sovereignty over the whole Arabian Peninsula, including Kuwait, but with the British protecting the tiny emirate the Ottomans were in no position to exercise their will. This treaty ensuring British protection of Kuwait remained in place until 1961.

Mubarek ruled for 19 years and is regarded as one of the most progressive emirs in the country's history. He began the process of changing his country from dusty desert towns into a thriving seaside community. During Mubarek's reign, the population of Kuwait tripled to 35,000. Mubarek opened the first schools and the first hospital in the country. Westerners were invited in to work as teachers and doctors. He created a civil service. The pearling and fishing trades during Mubarek's rule were prosperous.

He displayed a tolerance for other religions. Christian missionaries were welcomed in the country. So were Jews. Today, though, few Kuwaiti Christians remain and there are no Jews living in the country. Mubarek also gave sanctuary to members of the al-Saud family, which had lost a contest for control for territory known as the Hejaz in the peninsula south of Kuwait. The al-Saud had ruled this area in the 18th century and early years of the 19th century.

A Turkish helmet from the early 16th century. The Ottoman Turks built an enormous empire during the 16th and 17th centuries that included the Arabian Peninsula. Although Kuwait always considered itself independent of the Ottomans and under the rule of the al-Sabah family, the tiny kingdom maintained a good relationship with the Ottoman Empire. On behalf of the Turkish sultans, Kuwait's rulers administered Ottoman law to the eastern part of the Arabian Peninsula until the late 19th century.

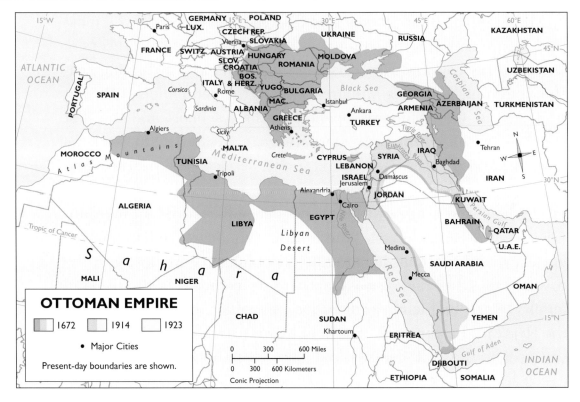

By 1672 the powerful Ottoman Empire controlled much of the Arabian Peninsula, as well as large parts of north Africa, central Asia, and eastern Europe. By the start of World War I (1914) however, the empire was concentrated in Turkey and the Middle East. After the war, former Ottoman territories were divided among the victorious allied powers and new Arab states were established. Several of these, including Saudi Arabia and Iraq, made no secret of their desire to annex Kuwait.

By the early 1900s, the influence and power of the Ottoman Turks was very much on the wane. The once-powerful Turkish empire was now regarded as the "Sick Man of Europe." The empire suffered from poverty at home, poor training for soldiers, and laziness by its leaders, who were more interested in fattening their own fortunes than in defending the Ottomans' vast foreign holdings. What's more, the sultans had to contend with revolution in their capital of Constantinople. During the first years of the 20th century, the powers of the Ottoman sultans had eroded to the point where they no longer could count on the loyalty of their troops.

In 1913, Great Britain and the Ottoman Turks signed a treaty known as the Anglo-Ottoman Convention, designating Kuwait an "autonomous *qada*," or district, of the Ottoman Empire. Decades later, these words would be at the root of Iraq's claims on Kuwait. Iraq insisted that Kuwait was ultimately subordinate to the Ottoman Empire, and that when the empire collapsed at the end of World War I Kuwait became subordinate to Iraq, which had been created from Ottoman territory. The Kuwaitis countered that the British-Turkish treaty was never ratified because the signers soon found themselves on opposite sides in World War I. When the Ottoman Empire ceased to exist after the war ended, the Kuwaitis maintained, the convention had no meaning.

In 1932, when Iraq won its independence from Great Britain, the country's Hashemite rulers protested Kuwait's autonomy. In 1958, when Qasim seized power in Iraq, he announced that he would no longer recognize the border between the two countries and moved troops into a position to strike. Later, of course, Saddam Hussein would make an even more daring claim on Kuwaiti territory.

THE AFTERMATH OF WORLD WAR I

In 1914, World War I erupted in Europe. The Ottoman Turks entered the war on the side of the Central Powers, which were led by Germany and Austria-Hungary. Great Britain realized it had the opportunity to drive the Turks out of the war by encouraging the Arabs to rise up against their long-hated oppressors. In return, the British promised to restore the Arab kingdoms following the war. In 1916, prompted by the British, Arab leaders in the Middle East staged the Great Arab Revolt against the Ottoman Turks. By the end of the war the Arabs had taken control of Jordan, Syria, and the Arabian Peninsula from the Ottomans.

Following the war, the victors carved up the former Ottoman territories. Arab states were created, but placed under British and

French domination. Soon, the al-Sauds gained control of the Hejaz territory they had previously controlled on the Arabian Peninsula. The country was renamed Saudi Arabia, and the new ruler, Abdul Aziz bin Abdul Rahman al-Saud, set out to build a kingdom that would encompass the entire peninsula. Although the Kuwaitis had given Abdul Aziz shelter during his years of exile, the Saudi ruler made it clear that he wanted his new kingdom to include Kuwait. The events that led up to the clash between the Kuwaitis and Saudis marks one of the few times in history that Kuwaitis took up arms in their own defense.

By 1920, the emir of Kuwait was Mubarek's son, Salim. To depose Salim, Abdul Aziz enlisted the aid of the *Ikhwan*, an elite corps of fanatic Muslim soldiers. On April 4, a garrison of Kuwaiti troops was attacked and massacred by the *Ikhwan*. A few soldiers managed to escape, and returned to Kuwait City where they reported the attack. Quickly, the Kuwaitis erected a new wall around their city (the old mud wall built in 1760 had long since collapsed). Every man, woman, and child in the city capable of working participated in the construction of the wall, and it was completed in just 60 days. The *Ikhwan* raiders apparently believed the wall was too great a hurdle to overcome, and instead directed their attack at the town of al-Jahra, about 20 miles east of Kuwait City.

A military post known as the Red Fort protected al-Jahra. Salim raised an army of Kuwaiti citizens and headed to al-Jahra. On October 10, the two armies clashed just outside the city.

Salim's volunteer army was no match for the *Ikhwan*. The Kuwaitis suffered terrible losses, and finally retreated into the safety of Red Fort. Salim's only hope now was to save Kuwait City. He believed that by drawing the *Ikhwan* into a prolonged siege at Red Fort, he could delay the assault on the Kuwait capital until the British could be summoned to intervene.

As it turned out, the British didn't have to do much to end the crisis. British warplanes flew over *Ikhwan* camps, dropping leaflets that warned the Ikhwan not to attack the capital. The British also rushed some warships to the Kuwait shoreline. A few heavy gun blasts aimed at the enemy camps sent the *Ikhwan* scattering. Some British marines actually landed ashore in Kuwait, but none found it necessary to fire their weapons. The *Ikhwan* retreated, and Kuwait's independence was maintained.

One of the reasons the European powers wished to maintain control over the Middle East is that even in the early years of the 20th century, the region was recognized as a source for a great amount of oil. As industry in the Western nations began relying more and more on the gasoline-fueled internal combustion engine, political leaders realized that a guaranteed source of oil would be vital to their countries' economies. The British also sought a source of diesel fuel for its ships, because the navy was essential for Britain to extend its power throughout its empire and the world.

The first oil well was sunk in Kuwait in 1936 in al-Bahara, north of Kuwait City. It was financed by a consortium composed of British and American businesses, including the U.S.-

A member of Kuwait's ruling al-Sabah family tours a British Petroleum (BP) refinery in England, circa 1956. Great Britain had long maintained strong ties with Kuwait; the discovery of oil in the kingdom made Kuwait even more strategically important to the British Empire in the decades after the end of the Second World War.

based Gulf Oil Company. The venture was named the Kuwait Oil Company. Although the al-Bahara well came up dry, further exploration turned up vast quantities of oil. Within two years, it was clear the tiny emirate was virtually floating on oil.

World War II erupted in 1939, forcing the Kuwait Oil Company to cease production until hostilities ended. Following the war, production resumed and by the early 1950s Kuwait was one of the major suppliers of oil to the West. The flood of money that poured into the country's treasury transformed Kuwait from a land of humble desert dwellers to an international economic dynamo. And from the start, the ruling family made a commitment to share the wealth with the people.

A pall of smoke hangs over a deserted street in Kuwait City shortly after the end of the Gulf War. Kuwait spent more than $160 billion to repair the damage done to the country during the Iraqi occupation.

In 1961, Kuwait gained its independence from Great Britian and became a member of the Arab League. The next year, on November 11, 1962, the country's constitution was ratified by the emir. Kuwait's first elected National Assembly was convened in 1963.

By the 1970s tremendous changes had taken place in Kuwait. Modern hotels, homes, and office buildings were erected in Kuwait City and other towns. Modern highways cut across the desert landscape. Museums and universities were built. Kuwaiti citizens were suddenly able to afford expensive cars and vacation homes in European resorts. Foreign workers were hired as housekeepers and other servants.

In 1976 the government of Kuwait **nationalized**, or took over, the major petroleum company in the country, Kuwait Oil Company (KOP). This would give Kuwait more control over the development of its oil resources. Eventually, KOP and other oil firms were integrated into the government-run Kuwait Petroleum Company (KPC). Oil production had been 5.9 million barrels in 1946; by 1980 Kuwait was producing more than 600 million barrels of oil a year.

But the oil wealth that had made Kuwait into a desert paradise incited ambitions among its neighbors. Iraq had long coveted Kuwaiti territory; it had opposed the country's entrance in the Arab League by arguing that Kuwait should be part of Iraq. Even though Kuwait supported Iraq in its war against Iran (1980–88), in the summer of 1990 Iraq invaded the emirate, leading to the 1991 Gulf War.

After the war Kuwait spent more than $160 billion to rebuild the country; today, Kuwait once again is a prosperous nation. In the aftermath of the Gulf War, the country cultivated closer ties with the United States, other western nations, and its Arab neighbors as a measure to prevent another strike by Iraq. In March 2002, Iraq signed a commitment with Kuwait in which it renounced its claim on the territory and promised never to invade the emirate again.

The oil refinery at Mina Abd Allah, Kuwait, at twilight. Petroleum-related income accounts for more than three-quarters of the government's revenue.

Politics, Religion, and the Economy

*T*he founding fathers wrote that their people should "strive [for] a better future in which the country enjoys greater prosperity and higher international standing, and in which also the citizens are provided with moral freedom, equality and social justice."

Those words are not found in the U.S. Constitution, although certainly they could be, as they reflect the will of a people whose main goal is to ensure equality and justice for all. Those words are included in the preamble to the Constitution of the State of Kuwait, which was signed by Emir Abdullah al-Salim al-Sabah on November 11, 1962. Kuwait is one of the few countries in the Arab world to be governed by a constitution that ensures the people a role in their government through the election of a National Assembly.

In the years since the oil boom brought riches to the tiny

emirate, Abdullah resolved to share the wealth of Kuwait with the people. Starting in the mid-1950s, Abdullah commenced an ambitious program to modernize Kuwait, ensuring his people a comfortable lifestyle. More than just the infrastructure was improved. Abdullah built schools and made education free. He built hospitals and made health care free. He built power plants and charged his people just pennies for the electricity that was fed into their homes. He enlarged the civil service and guaranteed Kuwaitis a job in the government if they couldn't find employment elsewhere. Most Kuwaitis found themselves working just a few hours a day.

There was more than just benevolence behind Abdullah's motives. Elsewhere in the Arab world change was taking place, often violently. In Iraq, Qasim had seized power after murdering the royal family. In Jordan, King Hussein came to power in 1953 after the assassination of his grandfather by a Palestinian and the abdication of his father Talal. King Hussein would spend most of the 1950s and early 1960s dodging attempts on his own life. In Egypt the 1949 truce with Israel following the Jewish state's war of independence touched off three years of rioting and assassinations that ended in 1952 with the exile of King Farouk. Army officers took command and, eventually, Colonel Gamal Abdel Nasser seized control of the government. Nasser would soon make known his pan-Arab vision of a single nation that would encompass all Arab states. It was a plan that appealed to many Arabs but was opposed by most of their leaders—particularly members of royal houses whose families had ruled for generations, like the al-Sabah.

Emir Abdullah aimed to buy the loyalty of his people not only with the luxuries of an easy life, but with a role in the government as well. Following Kuwait's independence from Great Britain, Abdullah signed a constitution that contained 183 articles—many of them granting freedoms and rights that could be found in the constitutions of Western democracies. "The system of government

Kuwaiti youths learn how to repair an engine in this 1952 photograph. During the 1950s Emir Abdullah al-Salim al-Sabah began using the revenues his country received from oil to provide educational training and job opportunities for Kuwaitis.

in Kuwait shall be democratic, under which sovereignty resides in the people, the source of all powers," declares Article 6. Article 9 of the constitution says: "All people are equal in human dignity and in public rights and duties before the law, without distinction as to race, origin, language, or religion." The constitution also contains provisions against illegal searches and seizures, the right of a fair trial, freedom of the press, freedom of assembly, and the right to petition—all rights that can be found in the U.S. Bill of Rights.

Make no mistake, though, there are some very significant differences between Kuwait's constitution and the set of laws one would find in a Western democracy. Kuwait is a monarchy—the laws written in 1962 established the emir as the chief executive of the government, and ensured that no one but a member of the al-Sabah family could serve as emir. What's more, the constitution specified that the emir himself would choose his successor, although the National Assembly is given the responsibility of confirming the heir apparent.

Kuwait's flag, adopted in 1961, is similar to the flag used by the Arabs during their 1916 revolt against the Turks. The colors are the same, but the Arab Revolt flag had a red triangle and black-green-white stripes, rather than a black trapezoid and green-white-red stripes. The flags of Jordan, Sudan, and the United Arab Emirates are also similar to the Arab Revolt flag.

Also, the constitution gives the emir power to dissolve the National Assembly. In essence, if the emir disagrees with the elected parliament, he can ignore it and rule on his own. Certainly, the idea of the president of the United States putting a padlock on Congress and ruling with no legislative branch is unthinkable. Nevertheless, in Kuwait the emirs reserved that right for themselves and have exercised it. In 1976, Emir Sabah al-Salim al-Sabah shut down the parliament after members of the National Assembly openly questioned the distribution of oil revenues, claiming the emir was showing favoritism to wealthy friends. The assembly did not meet again for five years. There have been occasional closures of parliament since then, including a closure in the 1980s prompted by an economic crisis and a two-year closure caused by the Iraqi invasion in 1990.

In recent years, women's **suffrage** has emerged as an issue in Kuwait. The 1962 constitution grants the right to vote only to male citizens. It should be pointed out that the U.S. Constitution, ratified in 1788, did not grant women the right to vote until 1920. Americans spent years debating the extension of suffrage to women. Kuwaitis have struggled with the issue as well.

Emir Jabir issued a decree in 1999 permitting women to vote and hold public office. Advocates of women's suffrage rejoiced, and many flocked to voter registration centers in February 2000 to sign up. "Every year . . . our request to register is rejected, but this time matters have changed," said Ma'asouma al-Mubarak, a female college professor in Kuwait and advocate for women's suffrage.

The victory was short-lived. The National Assembly rejected the emir's decree by a 32–30 vote. Women's suffragists took their case to the Constitutional Court, Kuwait's version of the Supreme Court. In January 2001, the court ruled against the suffragists, finding that only the National Assembly could change the law that would enable women the right to vote.

Women's rights activists have vowed to try again, but political observers in Kuwait believe that the National Assembly is becoming more conservative and, therefore, is unlikely to extend suffrage to women. During the past few years, Islamic fundamentalists have been elected to parliament. They adhere to a stricter

A view of downtown Kuwait City at night. The city is Kuwait's commercial and banking center, as well as the seat of government.

interpretation of the Qur'an and are unwilling to extend to women rights they believe are forbidden under Islamic law.

The growing movement of fundamentalism in Kuwait can be seen in Kuwaitis' feelings toward America. Following the expulsion of the Iraqis in 1991, Kuwait owed its continued existence as a nation to the United States. But 10 years later, Kuwaitis found themselves unwilling to support America with the same vigor as they had following the Gulf War.

In February 2002, a poll conducted by the Gallup organization found that 36 percent of Kuwaitis surveyed believed that the September 11, 2001, terrorist attacks on the World Trade Center and Pentagon were "morally justifiable." Just 17 percent of

Thousands of Kuwaiti men gathered in June 1999 to hear speaches by politicians just prior to the parliamentary election that year. Although the people of Kuwait do have a role in their government through their elected National Assembly, much of the power—including the authority to dissolve the assembly—rests with the emir.

Kuwaitis supported the United States in its war against the Taliban regime in Afghanistan, which had harbored Osama bin Laden and the al-Qaeda terrorist network. Many leaders of Kuwait society were puzzled by those results and openly questioned them, believing that the Gallup Organization had erred in the conduct of its poll. After all, they pointed out, most Kuwaitis own American cars, which they drive to shopping malls that feature such American businesses as Pizza Hut restaurants and Starbucks coffee shops. Gallup officials defended the poll, however, contending that the polling was accurate. Saud al-Sabah, a member of the royal family, insisted that the Kuwaiti people continue to support America. "Let me be quite clear," Saud told an American journalist in 2002. "We need you more than you need us."

RELIGION IN KUWAIT

The Bill of Rights in the U.S. Constitution guarantees freedom of religion, as does the Kuwait constitution. In America, however, there is no state religion, while in Kuwait Islam is designated as the official religion of the people. Article 2 of the Kuwait Constitution states: "The religion of the state is Islam, and the Islamic *Sharia* shall be a main source of legislation."

Sharia is Islamic law, but it is more than just a set of rules. *Sharia* spells out the moral goals of a community and covers a Muslim's religious, political, social, and private life. In an Islamic society, the courts look to the *Sharia* for guidance when interpreting the law and enforcing justice. The *Sharia* law is based on the Qur'an as well as other sources, including the Sunna, an early interpretation of the Qur'an written by Muhammad's followers.

Different Islamic nations apply *Sharia* to their societies differently. One of the most familiar examples of *Sharia* law in many Islamic countries is the custom requiring women to keep their faces covered in public. In Saudi Arabia and Iran, for example, women wear veils. In Afghanistan, during the ultraconservative Taliban regime, all women were required to wear the *burkha*—a costume that completely covers their bodies from head to toe, leaving only a small area in front of their eyes for them to see through. In Kuwait, *Sharia* is interpreted much more liberally; women do not have to cover their faces in public.

In many Islamic nations, people who break *Sharia* law risk brutal consequences. In Sudan, the sentence for armed robbery is the amputation of the right hand and left foot. Nigeria also amputates the hands of convicted thieves. In Afghanistan under the Taliban, homosexuals were executed. Even the manner in which they were put to death reflected the strong influence of *Sharia* on the country's society—they were stood against stone walls, which were then toppled over, crushing them under the falling rock. In other Islamic countries lawbreakers are stoned or whipped. Again, Kuwait's interpretation of *Sharia* is somewhat more liberal and corporal punishment is not employed.

There have been recent efforts in Kuwait to impose a more conservative interpretation of *Sharia*, however. National Assembly members have drafted legislation to adopt "physical torture" as punishment for such crimes as rape, adultery, and the consumption of alcoholic beverages. Punishment could include amputation of a thief's hand and the stoning to death of an adulterer. However, conservatives have not yet been able to obtain a majority of seats in the parliament and their efforts to enforce a stricter interpretation of *Sharia* have failed.

Of the 2.1 million residents of Kuwait, roughly 1.5 million of them follow the state religion, Islam. Virtually all of the approximately 1 million citizens of Kuwait are Muslims.

There are two major branches of Islam—Sunni Islam and Shi'a Islam—and both are represented in Kuwait. The Sunni and Shiite sects have been rivals for nearly 1,400 years. Following the death

(Right) Muslims pray in a mosque in Kuwait. (Below) Kuwait's State Mosque can accommodate 5,000 worshippers, with room for another 7,000 in a courtyard. Islam is the state religion, and Islamic law, or *Sharia*, is the basis of Kuwait's legal code.

of the Prophet Muhammad in A.D. 632, the Qur'an gave no clear method of succession for leadership of the faith. Two factions emerged in a contest for leadership. The Sunnis were led by the Umayyads, an aristocratic family from the Arabian city of Mecca. In Arabic, the word *Sunni* is derived from the term for "tradition." The Sunnis favored selection of the successor by Islamic leaders, who would elect the **caliph**.

A group of Muslims led by Ali, Muhammad's son-in-law, disagreed. They believed the caliph should be a member of Muhammad's family. They called themselves Shiites—a name drawn from the Arabic word for "partisan." Ali would eventually become the fourth caliph; when he was murdered the Shiites insisted the next caliph should be one of Ali's sons. The Sunnis prevailed, though, and the succession passed out of Ali's family. Sunnis have traditionally accepted secular leaders as the heads of their governments.

Today Sunnis make up the great majority of Muslims worldwide— about 85 percent of the total Islamic population of nearly 1 billion. More than two-thirds of Kuwaitis are Sunnis—over 700,000 citizens along with another 700,000 alien residents (mostly other Arabs who live and work in the country). The al-Sabahs and most other prominent families are Sunnis.

Kuwaiti Muslims pray in some 820 **mosques**, many of them quite old. The oldest mosque still standing in Kuwait is the Khalifa Mosque, which was constructed in 1737. The newer mosques, which were erected after the start of the oil boom, are often quite ornate. The State Mosque is the largest mosque in Kuwait. It was constructed of wood from India, limestone from Syria, marble from Italy, stained glass from France, and tiles from Morocco. The central building of the State Mosque covers some 150,000 square feet and can accommodate 5,000 worshippers. The dome over the mosque rises 150 feet from ground level.

The constitution says the "state safeguards the heritage of Islam." Those who follow other religions must register with government agencies in order to gain permission to worship within the country. Religions currently active in Kuwait include the Roman Catholic and Anglican churches and the National Evangelical Church of Kuwait, a Protestant denomination. Those religions are permitted to establish houses of worship in Kuwait. Smaller denominations are permitted to hold services in private homes. These groups include the Greek Orthodox, Armenian Orthodox,

Coptic Orthodox, and Greek Catholic churches. There are several other denominations that have not registered with the government (for example, Mormons, Hindus, Buddhists, and Sikhs). The Kuwaitis have not been very interested in enforcing the regulations or cracking down on their small worship services. However, Kuwaitis take a dim view of the recruitment of Muslims into those faiths. Missionaries are not permitted to preach to Muslims. The publishing or importation of Bibles or other non-Islamic religious books are carefully monitored by the Kuwaitis to ensure they stay out of Muslim hands. There are native-born non-Muslim Kuwaitis, but a 1980 law prohibits anyone other than a Muslim or a naturalized Muslim from becoming a citizen, meaning that the government intends to keep the non-Muslim population low. If a non-Muslim male marries a Muslim female, Kuwait's laws specify that he must convert to Islam. Women marrying Muslim men need not convert, but they are encouraged to do so.

The government protects Islam against criticism. In 2000, two female Kuwaiti authors, Alia Shuaib and Leila al-Othman, were convicted of writing books that were "blasphemous and obscene." According to prosecutors, the two women wrote books that were deemed insufficiently observant of Islamic norms. Shuaib's conviction was later overturned on appeal, but Othman's conviction on the charge of using obscene words was upheld. She was sentenced to two months in prison.

THE ECONOMY OF KUWAIT

Oil drives the Kuwait economy. Currently, the country produces about 1.8 million barrels of oil a day. The price of oil fluctuates, but over the past decade the price has averaged $21.50 a barrel. At that price, nearly $39 million a day has flowed into Kuwait's economy over a 10-year period. The United States and Japan buy most of Kuwait's oil.

The country's oil wealth and the willingness of the government to share some of that wealth with the people has meant that Kuwaitis enjoy one of the highest per capita incomes in the world. At about $18,000 a year per person, the Kuwaitis rank 31st in the world. For many years, they ranked among the top ten, but the depression in oil prices in the 1980s followed by the Gulf War and its drain on the country's economy drove down per capita income, and the Kuwaitis have yet to make a full recovery. Nevertheless, few Kuwaitis have faced financial difficulties.

Oil accounts for 95 percent of Kuwait's exports and 75 percent of the government's revenue. Other exports are ammonia, fertilizer, bricks, and cement, which are manufactured in Kuwait's factories.

Oil-related industries contribute 45 percent to Kuwait's gross domestic product (GDP), which is the market value of all goods and services produced in the country. In 1999, Kuwait's gross domestic product was about $29 billion. Another major chunk of the GDP in Kuwait is generated by its investments—the money Kuwaitis invest in foreign companies, banks, and bonds. Following the Gulf War, Kuwait drained as much as 70 percent of its foreign investments to rebuild the damage caused by the Iraqis.

Manufacturing accounts for 13 percent of the gross domestic product. In addition to the products that are exported, factories in Kuwait also produce paper products, furniture, table salt, and textiles. The government, which provides a job to any citizen in need of employment, accounts for 22 percent of the GDP. Agriculture has little impact on the economy of Kuwait—the country's few farms produce just 0.3 percent of the GDP.

The government realizes that the oil reserves will one day expire, and so there are some efforts underway to make the country less reliant on oil. Kuwaitis have invested heavily in the chemical industry. Also, Kuwait has launched a joint project with Qatar to build a steel plant.

The Economy of Kuwait

Gross domestic product (GDP*): $37.783 billion (2000)

GDP per capita: $18,030 (2000)

Inflation: 2.7%

Natural resources: petroleum, fish, shrimp, natural gas

Industry (60% of GDP): petroleum, petrochemicals, desalination, food processing, construction materials

Services (39.7% of GDP): transportation, communications, shipping, tourism

Agriculture (0.3% of GDP): practically no crops; fish

Foreign trade:

Imports—$7.4 billion: food, construction materials, vehicles and parts, clothing

Exports—$16.2 billion: oil and refined products, fertilizers

Currency exchange rate: 0.3023 Kuwaiti dinars = U.S. $1 (October 2002)

*GDP, or gross domestic product, is the total value of goods and services produced in a country annually. All figures 2001 estimates unless otherwise indicated. Sources: CIA World Factbook 2002; World Bank

Kuwaitis are heavily reliant on imports to provide them with many of the necessities and luxuries of life. Food, automobiles, appliances, computers, and other electronic devices, as well as all manner of items for the household, must be obtained from foreign manufacturers. In addition, Kuwait is dependent on foreign workers to do the jobs they won't do for themselves. Non-Kuwaitis perform virtually all the manual labor in Kuwait. Asians are common residents of Kuwait now, holding down many service sector jobs such as housekeepers and restaurant workers.

The inflation rate in Kuwait is estimated at less than 3 percent a year. The currency of Kuwait is the dinar. One Kuwait dinar equals about $3.30.

THE CRASH OF THE SOUK AL-MANAKH

During the late 1970s and early 1980s, many Kuwaitis grew foolish with their wealth, causing an economic catastrophe that cost their country billions of dollars.

In many countries, investors have established stock markets where shares of public corporations are bought and sold. The largest stock market in the world is the New York Stock Exchange, where the shares of more than 2,000 American companies are traded. There are other stock exchanges in the United States as well as Japan, Great Britain, France, Germany, and the other industrialized nations.

Investors in many small countries maintain stock exchanges as well. Kuwait has a stock exchange. Until 1982, investors also traded stocks on an unofficial exchange known as the Souk al-Manakh.

Many stock exchanges are strictly policed by government agencies that ensure only shares of legitimate companies are put on the market. In the

A gas station in Kuwait. The discovery of oil, and rapid growth in the oil industry after World War II, provided the impetus for modernization in the country. Today the people of Kuwait are among the wealthiest in the world.

United States, the Securities and Exchange Commission serves this function.

In the early 1980s, the Kuwaiti government provided little regulation of the Souk al-Manakh. As a result, the shares of many companies with few **assets** or potential to conduct legitimate business or earn profits were bought and sold on the Souk. In 1982, the Iran-Iraq War caused oil prices to drop, which meant money was short. That forced banks and other lenders to raise the interest rates on their loans, many of which had gone to investors who were buying stock on the Souk. Investors found themselves in need of cash and lacking confidence in the Souk al-Manakh companies to earn profits. They sold their shares at fire-sale prices, losing considerable sums of money because they had bought the shares at highly inflated prices. When the crash of the Souk occurred in August 1982, Kuwaiti investors owed their creditors some $92 billion.

It wasn't only wealthy Kuwaitis who lost money in the stock market crash. Many migrant Bedouins and other low-income residents had staked their life savings on speculative Souk al-Manakh trades, hoping to get rich quick.

Whenever Kuwaitis squandered their money in the past they looked to the government to bail them out of debt. This time, though, the al-Sabahs balked at instituting a government plan to assume everybody's debts. However, Emir Jabir did fall under criticism by the National Assembly for finding ways to pay off the debts of members of his family as well as close friends. The criticism reached such vocal proportions that the emir ordered the parliament closed down, which is his right under Kuwait's constitution.

Meanwhile, the country fell into a **recession**. Finally, the al-Sabahs approved a limited bailout, providing government money to shore up Kuwaiti banks, which were unable to collect on their debts because of the huge losses suffered by their borrowers.

Serving coffee is a sign of hospitality among Bedouins in Kuwait. Arabic coffee, a strong drink, is popular throughout the Middle East. Kuwaitis often follow traditional ceremonies when brewing and serving coffee to guests.

The People

K uwaitis are a minority in their own country. The approximately 1 million citizens of the country make up less than 50 percent of the population. The remaining 1.1 million people living in Kuwait are resident aliens. They include Arabs from other Middle Eastern countries; people from various countries of southern Asia and Africa; Europeans, Americans, and Australians; and thousands of other people whose nationality is "non-stated." Most of those people are *bidouns* (not to be confused with Bedouins)—Arabs who claim no nationality but have been refused citizenship in Kuwait. Some *bidouns* have lived in Kuwait for generations.

Ethnically, Arabs compose about 80 percent of the population while Asians compose about 9 percent. The remaining ethnic groups include blacks and whites mostly from Europe, Africa, Iran, and the United States.

PEOPLE WHO HAVE EVERYTHING

In the early 1950s, at the start of the oil boom, a visitor to Kuwait would have found a country slowly emerging from the only way of life it had known since the 1700s. At the time, Kuwait was just learning about its wealth. Oil wells had just started producing gushers. New cities were under construction to accommodate the thousands of workers who were expected to arrive to work in the oil fields. Highways were being built across deserts, skyscrapers were rising in cities, and huge oil tankers were anchored in Kuwait Bay.

And yet, a visitor didn't have to look far to find the old ways still very much in practice. In Kuwait Bay, teak sailboats known as "booms" carrying cargoes of dates, tea, and molasses were forced to navigate around the huge tankers. In port, fathers and sons worked hard alongside one another, with the older men teaching their off-spring the craft of shipbuilding. Heavy Indian teak logs, hand-sawn into one- and two-inch planks, lined the shore. Masts and spars were stacked in the shipbuilding yards. Blacksmiths working over open forges made straps to strengthen ships. Old men carving ship parts by hand sat in the sunshine on carved teak benches or on the mud-and-cement seats built into shop walls along the road.

If a visitor searched for that type of activity in Kuwait's seaport today, he would hardly find many Kuwaitis exhausting themselves in the desert sun with such vigorous labor. Virtually every native-born Kuwaiti has shared in the country's wealth; now, most Kuwaitis live comfortably. Kuwaitis can afford servants, air-conditioned homes, expensive automobiles, and holidays in foreign resorts. The government guarantees the education of their children.

Most Kuwaitis did not share directly in the wealth brought by the oil boom—the oil revenue went either into the government treasury or the personal bank accounts of members of the ruling al-Sabah family. Nevertheless, few Kuwaiti citizens found themselves

This map shows how most of Kuwait's people are concentrated in a small area along the coast. Kuwait City, with a population of 1.1 million, is the largest city in Kuwait. The average population density of Kuwait is 267 persons per square mile (103 persons per sq km).

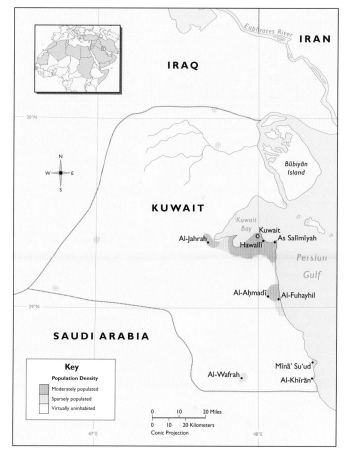

in need. Once the oil dollars started flowing, the government built schools and universities and decreed that education would be free to citizens. Health care is free. The government **subsidizes** food, meaning it is sold to the Kuwaiti people at a cost lower than they would pay in another country. Electric and water service, telephones, and other utilities are also subsidized. No taxes are collected in Kuwait.

Government jobs with guaranteed salaries are provided for any Kuwaiti who asks for one. Indeed, 90 percent of all employed Kuwaitis work in government jobs. Most jobs in Kuwait require workers to show up for just two or three hours a day. In fact, most Kuwaitis don't work. Just a quarter of Kuwait's citizens hold any type of job at all. In contrast, more than a million of the resident aliens in Kuwait hold down jobs.

The government provides all Kuwaiti newlyweds with a free house that includes two living rooms, five bedrooms, five bathrooms, and a room for the maid. If they wish to build their own

A Kuwaiti girl wears a traditional festival costume.

homes, the government gives them free land and an interest-free building loan.

Government leaders have long been concerned about the degeneration of a society in which the citizens have no worries about money and, therefore, no inclination to work. "Kuwaitis have become spoiled children. They want a job only if they can be directors or managers. The government would like to make hard work socially acceptable again. We have got to have Kuwaitis repairing cars, running retail shops, operating computers," said Fuad Mulla Hussein, secretary-general of the Kuwait Higher Planning Council. "The truth is we're not sure how to get Kuwaitis to work. How do you motivate someone who has everything?"

LEISURE ACTIVITIES

With so much money available and so much time on their hands, Kuwaitis are constantly searching for ways to fill their hours. Many have turned to western-style forms of entertainment. For example, wealthy Kuwaitis are members of the al-Shi'b, a yachting club that accommodates some 200 pleasure crafts. The club also includes a grassy park, theater, athletic facilities, restaurant, bowling alley, sauna, large pool, and tennis and basketball courts.

Each year, thousands of Kuwaitis flock to a Disneyland-style park known as Entertainment City, located 12 miles north of Kuwait City. The amusement park offers games, rides, and shows with three different themes: Arab World, International World, and Future World. Replicas of the Eiffel Tower, Leaning Tower of Pisa, and Dutch windmills have been erected in the park. Also, visitors can enjoy a mock sea journey that includes a trip through Sinbad the Sailor's cave.

Another entertainment center is Green Island, a 300-square mile artificial island created out of concrete and rocks. Beaches were fashioned by importing sand. More than 50,000 colorful shrubs and flowers were planted on Green Island. The entertainment center includes swimming pools, restaurants, and a theater with seating for 700 people. Young children can play in Kid's Castle, which includes playrooms, water channels, and waterfalls.

In Kuwait, bumpy rides can also be found outside of amusement parks. Camel racing remains a sport enjoyed by many Kuwaitis. In fact, there is a Camel Racing Club in the country that stages races

A group of Kuwaiti Boy Scouts wave the national flag.

in the desert near the town of Sulaibiya. The races are quite popular, and are often attended by diplomats and other prominent political figures. One big fan of the camel races is Emir Jabir, who subsidizes the club with a payment of some $360,000 a year.

Indeed, camel racing has become as competitive as thoroughbred horse racing in the United States. Camels bred especially for their speed are raised in Oman, Saudi Arabia, the United Arab Emirates, Sudan, and Kuwait. In Kuwait, owners have paid as much as $60,000 for a champion racing camel.

Usually, camel jockeys are young boys no more than 10 years old. As with horse racing in the United States, weight is an important factor so boys who aspire to be jockeys should be lean. Camel races don't start until 3 o'clock in the afternoon, which gives the young jockeys a chance to get home from school before saddling up their mounts. For children in Kuwait, school is a priority.

EDUCATION AND THE ARTS

Although Emir Mubarek built the first schools in Kuwait a century ago, education for children did not become manda-

The People of Kuwait

Population: 2,111,561 (includes 1,159,913 non-nationals)

Ethnic groups: Kuwaiti 45%, other Arab 35%, South Asian 9%, Iranian 4%, other 7%

Religions: Muslim 85% (Sunni 70%, Shi'a 30%); Christian, Hindu, Parsi, and other 15%

Age structure:
0–14 years: 28.3%
15–64 years: 69.2%
65 years and over: 2.5%

Population growth rate: 3.33%*

Birth rate: 21.84 births/1,000 population

Death rate: 2.46 deaths/1,000 population

Infant mortality rate: 10.87 deaths / 1,000 live births

Life expectancy at birth:
total population: 76.46 years
males: 75.56 years
females: 77.39 years

Total fertility rate: 3.14 children born/woman

Literacy: 78.6% (1995 est.)

*This rate reflects a return to pre-Gulf crisis immigration of expatriates.
All figures are 2002 estimates unless otherwise indicated.
Source: CIA World Factbook 2002

tory until 1965. Currently, there are about 300,000 students enrolled in Kuwait public schools. Of course, many Kuwaitis can afford to send their children to private schools. Some 8,000 Kuwaiti children attend classes in prestigious private academies.

Because the emirs of Kuwait used their country's wealth to build schools and universities, Kuwait has a low illiteracy rate—fewer than 5 percent of the citizens of Kuwait are believed to be illiterate. Of the total population, almost 80 percent of the people over age 15 can read and write.

Kuwait University was founded in 1966 with just 400 students. Today, more than 18,000 Kuwaitis attend classes at the sprawling campus, which employs nearly 1,000 teachers and professors. The university grants degrees in education, the sciences, economics, engineering, and Islamic studies.

Kuwait is home to several museums, many of which exhibit art, but Kuwaitis are not renowned for their artistic ability. Indeed, over the years, few Kuwaitis have attained fame as visual, musical, or dramatic artists.

TRADITIONAL LIFE

One tradition that Kuwaitis have kept alive over the generations is maintaining what is known as the *diwaniyah*, a place where Kuwaiti men gather to talk over matters of importance—events in the news, business, or issues involving friends and family members. Many men maintain *diwaniyahs* as rooms in their home; wealthy Kuwaitis will have separate structures erected near their homes to serve as *diwaniyahs*. Whether they are located in the home or in a separate building, the room is used for no other purpose.

Men attend the *diwaniyah* at set times every week. Traditionally, any male is welcome in a *diwaniyah*. The host serves snacks and coffee or tea. No subject is off-limits in the *diwaniyah*. Indeed,

Abdallah al-Ruwaished is Kuwait's favorite pop singer, and one of the most popular entertainers in the Arab world.

Kuwaitis can get quite outspoken and critical about their government while chatting in a *diwaniyah*, which may have been at the core of Emir Abdullah's thinking in 1962 when he ensured that freedom of speech would be a constitutional right in Kuwait.

Another old tradition that has been maintained in Kuwait is the Friday Mubarakiyah Market. Although there are shopping malls in Kuwait City, bargain hunters still enjoy buying goods at the open air market, known as the *souq*, where merchants display their wares spread out on carpets or under tents. The *souq*, which is on Fourth Ring Road in Kuwait City, is quite similar to the flea markets that bargain hunters can find in America.

At the *souq*, merchants expect to bargain with their customers. Carpets, camel saddles, soft drinks, jewelry, shoes, musical instruments, clothing, pots, candlesticks, cosmetics, lamps, and baskets are among the thousands of items for sale. Some vendors sell dogs, cats, and other pets, while many merchants sell goats and sheep.

Although western-style clothes such as blue jeans and business suits are available to Kuwaitis, many citizens of the country prefer more traditional outfits. Kuwaiti men often wear the *dishdashah*—a floor-length robe that is made of white cotton for summer and dark shades of wool for the winter. The flowing and often colorful headdress is known as the *kufyah*.

Men also wear *mesbah*, which are beads used for prayer. Often, the beads are known as "worry beads." The colorful beads are made of plastic, pearls, coral, turquoise, sandalwood, and amber. The *mesbah* derive their name from the Arabic word meaning "to praise and glorify God." The beads do have a religious use—they are flicked on their string during prayers. However, many Muslim men wear them as a fashion accessory and flick them as a pastime. Some men believe they can think clearly by concentrating on the beads and clearing their minds of other thoughts.

Many Kuwaiti women prefer western-style clothes and have not felt the need to wear the veil, known as

Shopper and trader bargain at Mubarakiyah Market, a traditional souq in Kuwait. Large sections of the market were destroyed during the Iraqi occupation.

the *hijab*, for decades. Also, Kuwaiti women have for the most part rejected the wearing of the *abaya*, a traditional black robe worn in public by Islamic women.

Another Islamic tradition that may be dying in Kuwait is the inclination of the emir to marry and divorce on a whim. Although authorized by the Qur'an, in recent years Kuwaitis have frowned on Emir Jabir's habit of taking wives and discarding them in rapid succession. It is believed that he has fathered at least 70 children. Although the emir has claimed that his marrying a young woman brings honor to her family and that he compensates his former wives after he divorces them, many Kuwaitis believe it is an old-world custom that has no place in a modern society.

THE FOOD

Thanks to their wealth, Kuwaitis have developed a taste for foreign dishes. French, Italian, Chinese, and Indian restaurants have popped up in the country. Also, Kuwaitis have their choice of many American fast-food restaurants, such as Kentucky Fried Chicken and Pizza Hut.

Still, traditional Arab dishes can be found on most tables in Kuwaiti homes. Kuwaitis usually eat a light breakfast. Their main meal of the day is lunch. Dinner is a small meal.

Popular dishes Kuwaitis enjoy include *shwarma*, a grilled meat sliced from a spit that is served in pita bread with salad; *hummus*, cooked chickpeas ground into a paste; *khouzi*, baked lamb stuffed with rice; *dolma*, rolled vine leaves stuffed with rice and meat; and *tabbouleh*, which is chopped parsley, tomato, onion and wheat.

Kuwaitis usually drink water or soft drinks with their meals, or *leban*, which is a diluted yogurt.

Meal times are regarded as an important part of the day in Kuwait. Food is served in abundance with many varieties offered, particularly when guests are present. Most Kuwaitis eat at western-

A fruit vendor in the Mubarakiyah Market, Kuwait City.

style dining tables, although some residents prefer a low table. Bedouins who eat in their traditional way sit on the floor, taking food from a communal platter using the fingers on their right hands.

Kuwaitis do not eat pork and they do not believe in consuming alcoholic beverages, both of which are forbidden under Islamic law. Many devoutly religious Kuwaitis will eat only meat and chicken that is slaughtered according to Islamic ritual. Such food is known as *halal*.

Kuwaitis love coffee, and they often serve it in large and ornate coffeepots with long beak-like spouts. The server pours the coffee into small china cups, just a little at a time. He'll keep pouring the coffee until the drinker jiggles the cup from side to side, giving the signal that he has enough. Arabic coffee—known as *qahwah Arabia*—is made by blending coffee with pods from the cardamom plant, which is similar to ginger.

Pedestrians walk past large buildings in Kuwait City, where more than half of the country's population lives.

Communities

Kuwait City is by far the largest city in Kuwait. In 2000, the population of the city and its suburbs was recorded at about 1.1 million people. In addition to being the country's largest city, it is certainly the oldest. Kuwait City dates back to the arrival of the Bani Utub tribe in the 18th century. Their tents were once pitched where skyscrapers and shopping malls stand today.

Kuwait City is the center of culture and the seat of government. Located in the city are the Seif Palace, which is where the emir carries out the business of the state, as well as the National Assembly, the Ministries Complex, Justice Center, and other government buildings. Also located in the city is Dasman Palace, which serves as the official residence of the emir.

Kuwait City sits along Kuwait Bay and, therefore, is an important center for the maritime industry in Kuwait, particularly for the oil tankers that transport the country's crude to Kuwait's trading partners in the United States, Japan, and other countries. Kuwait's largest banks are located in the city. These include the Bank of Kuwait and the Middle East and the National Bank of Kuwait.

Located just outside Kuwait City is Kuwait International Airport. The airport features a uniquely designed terminal—the building actually resembles an airplane. The passengers' hall is the plane's body, the civil aviation center is in the right wing, and a waiting area for VIP's can be found in the left wing. About 5 million passengers a year use the airport, which serves 38 airlines.

Kuwait's Telecommunications Center, which includes a 1,200-foot transmission tower known as Liberation Tower, is located in Kuwait City. It is the fourth-highest communications tower in the world after towers in Canada, Russia, and Germany. Liberation Tower is open to the public and includes a restaurant and observation platform.

Another set of tall structures in Kuwait is perhaps the country's most familiar landmark. Kuwait Towers, erected in 1979, are located on the Ras-Agoza cape in the northern part of the city. The complex includes three separate towers, the tallest of which is more than 600 feet high. It features restaurants and an observation deck located in globes that sit atop the tower. The second tower, which is nearly 500 feet high, contains a water tank that holds a million gallons of fresh water. The smallest of the three towers serves as an electrical power plant.

Two other large cities in Kuwait are al-Ahmadi, with some 435,000 residents, and al-Jahra, with about 150,000 residents.

Al-Ahmadi is a relatively new city, built to accommodate the oil industry. The community is just southwest of Kuwait City. It was planned in 1940 and completed in 1949, and is named after Emir al-Ahmad, who ruled the country when oil was first discovered. The

An ornate garden projects into the sea, with the lights of Kuwait City in the background.

city was designed to include western-style homes for the foreign workers who came to the Middle East to work for the Kuwait Oil Company. Indeed, with its suburban style streets and lush green lawns many Kuwaitis refer to the city as "Little America."

Al-Jahra is about 20 miles west of Kuwait City. The city is known as the location of Red Fort, where Emir Salim and his volunteer army made a stand against the *Ikhwan*. In recent years, it has become a center of industry in Kuwait. Another industrial city is al-Shuaibah, just south of Kuwait City. Al-Shuaibah features more than 30 large factories that manufacture such goods as paper, insulation, and glass. Fish processing plants and oil refineries are also located in al-Shuaibah.

FESTIVALS AND CELEBRATIONS

Whether they work hard at the task of rebuilding their country, or whether they are members of a leisure class created by the country's oil wealth, Kuwaitis are devout Muslims and, as such, they observe the holy month of Ramadan, the ninth month of the Islamic year. According to Muslim tradition, Ramadan was the month in which the Qur'an was revealed to Muhammad. During Ramadan, Muslims abstain from food and drink during the daylight hours and are encouraged to devote more time to meditation, strengthening their relationships with friends and family members, and studying the Qur'an. At night, people often stay up late socializing.

The last night of Ramadan is known as *Laylat al-Qadr*, or "Night of Power." It is significant because it marks the revelation of the first holy verse of the Qur'an to the prophet. Prayer services held in the State Mosque in Kuwait City on *Laylat al-Qadr* draw thousands of worshippers.

Ramadan is also a time of gift-giving. During the final three days of the month, Muslims in Kuwait celebrate by exchanging gifts and

Children in both traditional and Western dress take part in National Day festivities.

new clothes, and by visiting one another's homes. This period is known as Eid al-Fitr. Children receive "Eidah," money given by older relatives during the Eid. It is also tradition for a lamb to be slaughtered during the Eid, and for families and friends to gather for a great feast. Men also perform a ceremonial sword dance known as *Ardha*.

Other religious holidays include days that mark the birth of the prophet and the day of his ascension, as well as the four-day Eid al-Adha, which is the feast of sacrifice that also marks completion of the annual *hajj* period of pilgrimage to Mecca. The dates of Islamic holidays change each year according to the *Hijra*, a calendar based on the lunar cycle.

Secular holidays celebrated in Kuwait include New Year's Day, which falls on January 1; Kuwait National Day on February 25; and Kuwait Liberation Day on February 26. Kuwait National Day celebrates the country's independence from Great Britain in 1961, and Kuwait Liberation Day marks the end of the Gulf War in 1991.

In Kuwait, the weekend is regarded as Thursday and Friday, and that's when most Kuwaitis take their days off from work. Exceptions include workers in oil companies and banks, whose businesses must keep in step with the Western world. Banks and oil companies typically give their workers off Fridays and Saturdays.

A U.S. Marine sergeant speaks in Arabic with a Bedouin shepherd during a training exercise in 1997. Thousands of U.S. soldiers remained stationed in Kuwait in the years after the 1991 Gulf War.

Foreign Relations

Kuwait's importance in the world, and its relationships with foreign nations, center around its most important resource: oil.

By the middle of the 19th century, industry in America and Europe was in desperate need of oil. The fuel wasn't needed to run machinery in the factories or power automobiles—the internal combustion engine had not yet been invented. Nevertheless, the demands of production required some factories to run 24 hours a day. If employees were needed to work at night, it meant they would need to see what they were doing. As such, there was a tremendous need for oil to light lamps. Whale oil had been used in lamps for decades, but it was regarded as too expensive by industrial leaders who needed to keep the cost of running the factories low. Taking oil out of the ground was certainly not a new concept; over the years, whenever surface deposits of oil had been found people made use of it, mostly as a waterproofing material.

In 1859 Edwin L. Drake drilled the first commercially successful oil well in Titusville, Pennsylvania. Drake drilled down just 69 feet before striking oil. Drake's modest well marked the beginning of an industry that would come to dominate the world economy and dictate foreign policy between nations.

Just over a century after Drake struck oil in Titusville, diplomats from Kuwait, Iran, Iraq, Saudi Arabia, and Venezuela met in Baghdad to form the Organization of Petroleum Exporting Countries, or OPEC. Currently, OPEC—which has since expanded to 11 nations—possesses about 75 percent of the world's oil supply. Members of the organization seek to control the price of crude oil, the raw product that is pumped out of the ground and refined into gasoline, lubricants, and other products (many plastics, for example, are petroleum-based). In order to control prices, the members of OPEC must all agree to charge the same price for crude oil, which is sold by the barrel. They must decide among themselves how much oil to produce and then stick to the **quotas** they set.

Certainly, there are other places to obtain oil than the OPEC nations. The United States, Canada, Mexico, Russia, and Norway are also oil producers. Clearly, though, OPEC is a major force in the worldwide price of oil and, therefore, has a huge impact on the world economy.

Over the years, OPEC's problem has been that the members have often agreed to maintain production quotas, and then have broken their promises for selfish reasons. Obviously, the other members of the cartel will be hurt if one member suddenly floods the market with oil. That will cause prices to drop since oil, as a commodity, is subject to the basic law of supply and demand: if a commodity is in short supply, and there is a great demand for it,

Saud Nasser al-Sabah (left), Kuwait's Minister of Petroleum, listens during a 2000 meeting of the Organization of Petroleum Exporting Countries (OPEC) in Caracas, Venezuela. Seated with him are Saudi Crown Prince Abdullah and the Emir of Qatar, Sheikh Hamad Ben Khalifa Ben Hamed al-Thani. The 11 nations that are members of OPEC control about 75 percent of the world's known oil reserves.

people are willing to pay more to obtain it. When one member of the cartel suddenly and unexpectedly produces more oil than their OPEC quota, the price of oil will drop beyond the control of the group. The OPEC member making the most money in such a circumstance is the member that cheated, since that country is not restrained by production quotas and is pumping out the most oil.

In the late 1980s, the Kuwaitis were accused by Saddam Hussein of breaking the OPEC production quota and flooding the market with oil, which had a devastating impact on the economy of Iraq. That is one reason Saddam felt justified in launching the invasion of Kuwait that led to the Gulf War.

CONTROL OF THE OIL INDUSTRY

When oil production in the Middle East began again following World War II, the host nations had little say in where or how the wells were drilled. Following the war, the Arab nations did not have the money, the technology, or the skilled workers needed to find and drill for oil. They were forced to agree to partnerships with the Western oil companies. They signed so-called "fifty-fifty" deals with the oil companies, splitting the profits from the oil fields with the companies, most of which were American or British.

Middle East oil was abundant, of high quality, and inexpensive to extract and transport. Soon, worldwide oil prices started dropping—much to the dismay of American oil producers, mostly in Texas. What's more, American political leaders worried about becoming too dependent on foreign oil. They believed that if America relied too heavily on an unsteady foreign regime for its oil, and that a coup or political assassination suddenly shut down the oil supply, the national security of America could be threatened. And so, to ease the price pressure on domestic producers and to lessen the reliance on foreign oil, President Dwight D. Eisenhower ordered a limit on oil imports. That kept the international price of oil artificially high.

Meanwhile, in the Middle East, the new regimes bristled under the fifty-fifty deals. The first break with the fifty-fifty system occurred in 1951, when Iranian Prime Minister Mohammed Mossadeq nationalized all oil operations in his country. It meant that Iran no longer intended to share the profits with private companies from America and Britain. Two years later, Mossadeq forced Iran's ruler, Shah Mohammed Reza Pahlavi, from power. The U.S. Central Intelligence Agency (CIA) then assisted a coup that toppled Mossadeq and gave control back to the shah. The shah maintained a pro-Western government until 1979, when Islamic fundamentalist followers of Ayatollah Khomeini drove him out.

Another factor leading to the anger of Middle East leaders was the policy of American and European oil companies to pay the 50 percent royalties on what was known as the "posted" price for crude rather than the true market price. In essence, the oil companies fixed the posted price at whatever price they decided to pay—usually, much less than the market price of oil. In other words, the oil companies were cheating the host countries.

In 1959, the British Petroleum Company unilaterally cut the posted price by 10 percent. That set off a wave of anger in the Middle East. After a second cut in the posted price in 1960, the major oil producing nations formed OPEC.

Now, the OPEC countries could set the price of oil—at least in theory. The reality was not so simple. First, OPEC formed at a time when there was an oil glut, meaning oil had already been produced in such generous amounts that it would take several years for demand to rise. Next, the OPEC members were hesitant to cut production because in the 1950s many of them had started ambitious public improvement and development projects that were still underway and, therefore, in need of capital. Kuwait, for example, was overseeing a tremendous building program of highways, hospitals, skyscrapers, schools, desalinization plants, and shipyards.

Finally, the OPEC members did not trust each other, or their neighbors. Iraq had, after all, just threatened Kuwait with troop movements near the border. The Saudis distrusted the Egyptians, who were not OPEC members but, nevertheless, held considerable influence throughout the Arab world and were urging the creation of a pan-Arab state.

In Kuwait, national leaders took steps to finally sever their ties with Great Britain. The treaty signed by Mubarek in 1899 was replaced by a new treaty in 1961 that granted Kuwait full independence. Now responsible for their own security, the Kuwaitis raised an army of 7,000 soldiers, composed mostly of Bedouins. As for foreign policy, the emir, Abdullah Jabir al-Sabah, conducted diplomacy mostly with the country's checkbook. By 1965, Kuwait had loaned $14 million each to Nigeria, Lebanon, and Sudan, $28 million to Morocco, $140 million to Egypt, and $84 million to Iraq. Emir Abdullah's government financed highways, railroads, factories, power plants, and irrigation projects in 15 foreign countries. Asked by a reporter whether he considered his country secure from invasion, the emir responded, "We have no fears and no worries."

OIL CRISES AND GULF WARFARE

OPEC first flexed its muscles in 1973. The Middle East states restricted production of oil for Western nations, including the United States, which had supported Israel during the October 1973 Yom Kippur War against Egypt and Syria.

The efforts by the Arab members of OPEC to target the U.S. and the Netherlands for their support of Israel was ineffective because the major oil companies spread the shortage evenly. Nontheless, "panic buying" created artificial shortages at the pump, which

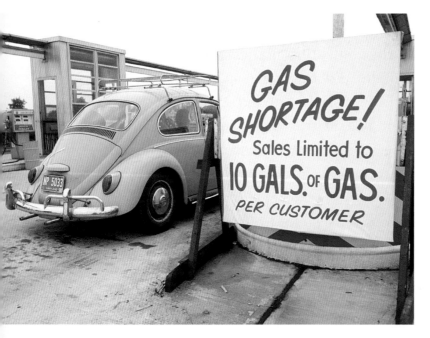

A sign at a Connecticut service station, 1974, cautions customers that their gas purchase will be rationed. During the Arab oil embargo, the price of a barrel of oil quadrupled, and long lines were common at gas stations in the United States and throughout the Western world.

caused prices to spike. Before the war, the price of crude oil was about $3 a barrel. During the embargo, the price rose to $12 a barrel. The Arab oil embargo thrust the Western nations into a recession and drove up the price of gasoline at the pump to more than $1 a gallon. In addition, to obtain a tank of gasoline motorists in many American cities were forced to wait in long lines, or buy gasoline only on certain days.

In 1979, the shah was overthrown in Iran. The fundamentalist regime that took power sent shock waves throughout the Arab world. Ayatollah Khomeini and his Shiite followers founded a state that would be run largely according to Islamic law and a strict interpretation of the Qur'an. What's more, the Iranians expressed a deep hatred for America, blaming the United States for its support of the shah's government. Shortly after the fundamentalists took power, student radicals stormed the U.S. embassy in Teheran and took 52 embassy workers hostage, holding them for 444 days.

A year later, war broke out between Iran and Iraq. The exact cause of the war has long been debated, but there is no question the two nations had been hostile to one another for years. One reason for the hostility is that Iraq was led by Sunni Muslims while Iran's leaders are Shiite Muslims. Also, in Iraq Saddam came to power in a secular movement and sought military aid from the Soviet Union— a country ruled by communism, where the state's position on religion was official **atheism**. The deeply religious clerics running Iran's government bristled at the thought of Muslims making an alliance with an atheist regime. During his years in exile from Iran Khomeini spent time in Iraq, where he urged the country's Shiite population to overthrow Saddam Hussein's government. Saddam responded by ordering a ruthless crackdown on Iraqi Shiites and sending aid to Sunni dissidents in Iran.

Throughout 1980, the two sides skirmished along their common border. In April, an Iranian-backed rebel group tried to assassinate

Iraqi Foreign Minister Tariq Aziz. In response, Saddam expelled hundreds of Shiites and executed a Shiite cleric. On September 17, Saddam declared the Shatt al-Arab River the property of Iraq; the river separates the two countries along their extreme southern border. Five days later, Iraq invaded Iran.

Sitting nervously in the middle of all this, virtually surrounded by hostile neighbors, were the Kuwaitis. Iran warned the other Gulf States to stay out of the conflict, but the Kuwaitis decided to support Iraq. The al-Sabah family had never been comfortable with Saddam Hussein in control of Iraq, but they felt they had more to fear from Iran, which threatened to export Islamic revolutionaries to their country and overthrow the al-Sabah regime just as they had overthrown the government of the Shah. Soon, Kuwait's economic aid to Iraq reached $1 billion a year. Saddam valued the Kuwaitis' help because the war against Iran soon bankrupted his country. To continue waging the battle, he needed financial aid from the other oil states as well.

By 1983, the Iraqi air force started doing serious damage to Iranian shipping. Iran responded by threatening to close the Persian Gulf—a circumstance that would be disastrous to Kuwait, because its fleet of oil tankers needed to sail through the gulf to reach the Indian Ocean. A small force of Iranian warships stationed in the narrow Strait of Hormuz would be sufficient to turn back the tankers. Not only would Kuwait be prevented from exporting its oil, but the people of the tiny emirate would be completely at the mercy of Iran. Kuwait was totally reliant on food and other supplies brought by ships sailing through the gulf.

A few months later Iran started attacking commercial shipping in the gulf, including vessels sailing under the flag of Kuwait. "At first, we thought Iran was trying to put pressure on us to persuade Iraq to let up, though we have no power over the Iraqis," Saoud al-Osaimi, minister of state for foreign affairs for Kuwait, later recalled. "We talked to the Iranians in an attempt to get them to change this policy. We talked directly, and we used intermediaries . . . finally, through the United Nations, we got the Security Council to pass Resolution 552, which called on Iran to stop attacking the harbors and boats of countries not involved in the war. But none of these efforts worked. In fact, for us things became worse at the end of 1985, when Iran began singling out Kuwaiti ships, especially our tankers, for attack."

Meanwhile, the Iranians were stepping up pressure inside Kuwait. In 1983, Lebanese and Iraqi Shiite militants, taking their orders from Iran's leader, Ayatollah Khomeini, bombed the American and French embassies in Kuwait City. Six people were killed and 80 wounded in the attacks.

By late 1986, neither Iran nor Iraq seemed interested in ending the war. The Kuwaitis were now certain that if they didn't act, the fighting would spread to their shores. Certainly, they feared for the safety of their shipping.

INVOLVEMENT OF THE SUPERPOWERS

The Kuwaitis' first preference would have been to seek the assistance of the United States. Iran still regarded America as its mortal enemy—the "Great Satan." What's more, since the start of the war the American president, Ronald Reagan, had made it known that the U.S. hoped the Iraqis would win. In 1984, the United States reestablished diplomatic relations with Iraq, which had been broken off since 1967, when America backed Israel in the Six Day War against the Arab states.

Nevertheless, the Americans gave the Kuwaitis reason to doubt their commitment. It seemed to the Kuwaitis that the U.S. government had been in no hurry to negotiate the release of American hostages snatched off the streets in Lebanon by agents of the ayatollah. Also, the Kuwaitis were puzzled as to why the Americans took no retaliatory action against Iran following the Shiite terrorist attack on the U.S. Embassy in Kuwait City. Finally, in 1986, a scandal erupted in the United States: to win freedom for the hostages in Lebanon, the Reagan Administration had apparently been willing to indirectly supply arms to the Iranians for use in the war against Iraq.

To the Kuwaitis, the arms-for-hostages deal had confirmed their suspicions: the Americans were on the ayatollah's side. So to seek protection for its shipping, Kuwait approached the Soviet Union— at the time, the world's other superpower.

In late 1986, the Kuwaitis opened talks with the Soviets, but the talks did not get very far. The Soviets were preoccupied with their own war; since 1979, they had been occupying Afghanistan, and the resistance by Afghan freedom fighters had evolved into a long and bloody struggle. What's more, when Reagan learned the Kuwaitis had approached the Soviets, he immediately offered American help. Reagan was a virulent anti-communist and had made it the mission of his administration to eliminate the Soviet Union's influence in the world. Certainly, Reagan wasn't going to allow Soviet ships to control the oil trade in the Persian Gulf.

In early 1987, Reagan announced that the fleet of 11 Kuwaiti oil tankers would be "reflagged" as American vessels. It meant that the ships would sail under the American flag, and that any attack on those ships would be regarded as an attack on American ships. To protect the tankers, Reagan dispatched 34 U.S. Navy ships to the Persian Gulf. France, Great Britain, Italy, and Belgium sent warships to the gulf as well.

Still, the Iranians pursued the war into Kuwait. Kuwaiti soldiers stationed on the island of Bubiyan were fired on by Iranian forces. Meanwhile, Iran laid mines in the Persian Gulf. When an American warship hit a mine and was damaged, the U.S. Navy took action. Two Iranian oil platforms erected in the gulf were attacked and

A Kuwaiti oil tanker is escorted through the Persian Gulf by an American warship, August 1987. When Iran threatened Kuwaiti shipping at the height of the Iran-Iraq War, the United States sent its navy to intervene.

destroyed by American ships. When the Iranian navy arrived to repel the invasion, a sea battle ensued. Iran lost six ships in the melee.

Meanwhile, worldwide oil prices reached a peak in the early 1980s, but soon began falling. With two key members of OPEC in a state of war, the group was hardly in a position to stand firm on prices or production quotas. During the 1980s, both the Saudis and Kuwaitis violated their production quotas, anxious to secure greater market shares. During the war, Kuwait's quota was 1.5 million barrels of crude a day, but the tiny emirate was actually pumping 2.4 million barrels a day.

The Iraq-Iran War ended in a stalemate in 1988. The war had inflicted terrible losses on both countries, but particularly on Iraq, both socially and economically. It is believed that 120,000 Iraqis lost their lives in the fighting. When the war started, Iraq held foreign investments totaling some $35 billion; by the time the truce was declared, the country owed $40 billion to the foreign governments that had advanced loans to Saddam during the fighting. In Iraq, there were no jobs awaiting the returning soldiers. Inflation soared.

THE GULF WAR

Saddam was anxious to rebuild his country and appealed to the Arab world for help. He insisted that he had waged the war for the common good of all Arab regimes, arguing that the Iraqis had single-handedly stopped the spread of the fundamentalist Islamic revolution that had toppled the shah. Saddam asked the leaders of the oil states to forgive the loans they had made to his country during the war and to authorize new loans to Iraq totaling $30 billion. He found the oil sheiks cold to his appeals, though, particularly the Kuwaitis.

Saddam was incensed at Kuwait, which he blamed for violating its OPEC production quotas. Also, Saddam accused the Kuwaitis of stealing oil from Iraq—he alleged that the Kuwaitis had dug slant wells in the Ar Rumaylah oil field along the Iraq border, pumping Iraqi oil out of the ground on the Kuwait side of the border.

His demands were rejected. For months, he kept up the pressure on the other Arab leaders, but they refused to consider the Iraqi dictator's pleas. Most obstinate, it seemed, were the al-Sabah rulers of Kuwait, who seemed to have little fear of the dictator. Later, the al-Sabahs conceded that they had underestimated Saddam's intentions, believing then that if he did take direct military action it would amount to no more than a brief and mostly symbolic invasion of the sparsely populated Bubiyan and Warbah islands. Iraq had made claims to those islands in the past.

Saddam continued to insist that he had no intentions to invade Kuwait or any other Arab state—a promise he eventually broke on August 2, 1990. In the final few days before the Iraqi army crossed the border into Kuwait, several Arab leaders met with Saddam and the al-Sabahs to see if they could mediate the dispute. One of those leaders was King Hussein of Jordan, who had maintained friendly relations with Saddam.

On July 30, King Hussein arrived in Baghdad to speak with Saddam, who assured him that he had no intention of attacking the Kuwaitis. The king accepted Saddam's word, and then flew on to Kuwait. He met with Crown Prince Saad al-Abdallah al-Sabah, and told the Kuwaiti leader that Saddam was angry, but had said he would not attack.

After Hussein returned to Jordan on July 31, he telephoned President George H.W. Bush in Washington and advised him of the military threat posed by Iraq to Kuwait. Two days later, Iraqi troops crossed the border and attacked Kuwait.

The invasion proved to be a disaster for Iraq. The United States mobilized an international coalition, which attacked Iraq on January 17, 1991. The fighting was over in less than 60 days. "Operation Desert Storm" ousted the Iraqis from Kuwait and drove them back to Baghdad, but not before the Iraqis had plundered and vandalized Kuwait cities and set fire to hundreds of oil wells. Bush elected not to pursue the war past the eviction of the Iraqis from Kuwait, a decision America and its Western allies would soon regret as Saddam slowly re-armed his military and backed terrorist groups.

Kuwaitis suffered terribly in the war, in both human and financial terms. More than 15,000 citizens of the country were taken captive, and the Iraqis tortured most. Some 1,000 Kuwaiti women

Looting and destruction of buildings was common during the Iraqi occupation of Kuwait. Pictured is the Regency Hotel, before and after Iraqi soldiers set it on fire.

were raped. About 350 Kuwaitis died in prison, usually after gruesome torture at the hands of the invaders. Some 600 Kuwaiti soldiers were captured by the Iraqis and sent back to Iraq as prisoners of war. Their fate remains unknown.

Few Kuwaitis died defending their country in the first days of the war. Kuwaiti soldiers put up little resistance against the invaders. One of the few fights between Kuwaitis and Iraqis occurred just after the Iraqis crossed the border. Fahd al-Ahmad al-Sabah, brother of Emir Jabir, fought alongside his troops in a skirmish at the Dasman Palace, the emir's official residence. The Iraqis easily overran the defenders, and Fahd was killed. He was the only member of the royal family to die defending his country.

About 400,000 Kuwaitis fled the country during the war—including the emir and other members of the al-Sabah family, who remained in Saudi Arabia until just after the Iraqis were ousted.

The Kuwaitis returned to their homes following liberation, but many other residents chose to remain out of the country.

Prior to the invasion, about 400,000 Palestinians had lived in Kuwait, providing the Kuwaitis with a labor force for the country's manual and menial jobs. A year after the war, the Palestinian population numbered just 30,000. Palestinian leader Yasir Arafat had backed Saddam during the war; following liberation, the Kuwaitis exhibited considerable hostility toward Palestinians, and they were made to feel no longer welcome in the country.

Overall, the population of Kuwait before the invasion was about 2.1 million people. A year after liberation, the population had dropped by about a million people. The population has since recov-

U.S. President George H.W. Bush meets with American soldiers stationed in Saudi Arabia, November 1990. Under Bush's leadership an international coalition was formed in the summer and fall of 1990 to force Iraqi troops out of Kuwait.

> Immediately following liberation, the Kuwaitis changed the name of Baghdad Street in Kuwait City to George Bush Street to honor the American president who ordered the attack on the Iraqis. Also, many Kuwaiti children born shortly after liberation were named Bush by their parents.

ered as Asians emigrated to Kuwait, replacing the Palestinians in the country's workforce.

There was, of course, a great financial loss to the Kuwaitis as well. Following liberation, the Kuwaitis agreed to pay the United States $16.5 billion for the cost of Operation Desert Storm. The royal family ordered the government to assume all consumer and commercial debt in the country, which amounted to the staggering total of $30 billion. It meant that no Kuwaiti citizen or business owner would be burdened by debt while trying to rebuild his home or company. The list of losses went on and on. Cost of repairing damage to the oil wells was $75 billion. Cost of repairing the infrastructure—the highways, power plants, and utilities—amounted to $20 billion. Overall, it was estimated that final cost of the war and reconstruction in Kuwait totaled more than $160 billion.

The Kuwaitis spent what was needed to rebuild their country. And in the time it took to repair the damage, the citizens of the tiny desert nation built a new Kuwait: a country that learned from its past mistakes, eager to offer a fresh start to its people.

KUWAIT TODAY

Since the end of the Gulf War, Kuwait has worked to maintain ties and increase trade with coalition member nations from around the world. These include the United States and Great Britain, as well as France, China, Russia, and other major countries in both Asia and the West.

At the same time, Kuwait has been an important part of the Arab world. It has strengthened its ties with the members of the Gulf Cooperation Council (GCC)—Saudi Arabia, Bahrain, Qatar, Oman, and the United Arab Emirates—and has established a closer relationship with such Arab countries as Egypt, Syria, Morocco, and Lebanon—all of which were involved in the coalition against Iraq. Kuwait is a member of the Arab League of Nations, and with Saudi Arabia is a major shareholder in the Arab Fund for Economic Development, which has paid for development projects throughout the Middle East.

The cultivating of alliances has been part of a strategy to protect Kuwait from future Iraqi aggression. So far this strategy has worked. In November 1994, Iraq gave up its claims to Kuwait and to the Bubiyan and Warbah islands when it formally accepted borders established by the United Nations. And in March 2002, Iraq signed an agreement with Kuwait in which it promised to respect the country's sovereignty.

This agreement, negotiated by Kuwait's GCC neighbors Qatar and Oman, occurred at an Arab League summit in Lebanon.

A Kuwaiti and a U.S. soldier work together to prepare an explosive during Exercise Bright Star 98, This was a field training exercise in Egypt. The U.S. military worked with forces from Kuwait, Egypt, the United Arab Emirates, France, Italy, and the United Kingdom, in order to improve military readiness and coalition interoperability in the region.

The U.S. Secretary of Defense, Donald Rumsfeld, meets in Kuwait City with Foreign Minister Sabah al-Ahmad al-Sabah in June 2002. Rumsfield was on a 10-day tour of nine countries to meet with senior leaders and visit with U.S. troops deployed abroad.

Another major development at the meeting was a peace initiative by Saudi Prince Abdullah to resolve the violent conflict between the state of Israel and Palestinian Arabs.

During the 1990s Kuwait was involved in attempts to end the Israeli-Palestinian clash. Despite Palestinian support of Iraq during the Gulf War, in 1994, Kuwait donated $25 million in development aid to the Palestinian Authority, the recognized government established by the Oslo Accords a year earlier. Kuwait also was one of the few Arab nations that allowed trade with Israel.

Though Kuwait maintains strong ties with the United States, it has opposed the U.S. on certain matters. For example, in 2002 when American leaders began discussing the possibility of an attack that would remove Saddam Hussein from power, the Kuwaiti government was opposed. When U.S. Vice President Dick Cheney toured the Arab world in the spring of 2002, the Kuwaitis—as well as every other Arab leader he met—rejected military action against Iraq. Kuwait and other Arab countries did call on Saddam to open his country to U.N. weapons inspectors, to prove that he was not developing biological, nuclear, or chemical weapons of mass destruction. Under this pressure, Iraq allowed U.N. weapons inspectors into the country in late 2002.

Today, Kuwait remains a key ally of the United States. The tiny country of fewer than a million citizens has a great influence on peace in the Middle East, as well as on the world's economy. It remains to be seen whether the U.S. and its Western allies can influence the al-Sabah family to move their country toward democracy and a more open society.

CHRONOLOGY

circa 2300 B.C.: The Dilmun civilization, based in Bahrain, establishes a settlement on Failaka Island.

300 B.C.: Greeks establish a colony on the Kuwait island of Failaka, naming it Ikaros.

A.D. 570: about this time, the Prophet Muhammad is born in Mecca on the Arabian peninsula; some 40 years later he will have a vision of the angel Gabriel, giving birth to the Islamic faith.

1300s: founding of the Ottoman dynasty, which will soon conquer the Arabian peninsula.

1700s: Bani Utub tribe migrates across the Arabian peninsula to a settlement along the Persian Gulf.

1756: Sabah bin Jabir bin Adhbi becomes first emir of the Bani Utub settlement.

1760: Al-Sabahs erect a wall around their settlement, prompting settlers to name it "Kuwait," an Arabic term for "Little Fort."

1896: Emir Muhammad assassinated by his half-brother Mubarek, who three years later signs a treaty with Great Britain ensuring British protection for Kuwait.

1916: Great Arab Revolt liberates Arabian peninsula from Ottoman Turk rule.

1920: Emir Salim defends his country at Red Fort against the *Ikhwan*, a fierce warrior tribe enlisted by Saudi ruler Abdul Aziz to conquer Kuwait.

1936: First oil well drilled in Kuwait at al-Bahara, north of Kuwait City.

1960: Kuwait, Iran, Iraq, Saudi Arabia and Venezuela form the Organization of Petroleum Exporting Countries (OPEC).

1961: Iraqi leader Abd al-Karim Qasim moves troops to the Kuwait border and threatens an invasion; Kuwait granted full independence by Great Britain.

1962: Emir Abdullah signs a constitution giving limited democracy to Kuwaitis.

1973: OPEC cuts production to United States and other western nations that backed Israel in the Yom Kippur War.

1980: War breaks out between Iraq and Iran threatening the security of Kuwait, which sends economic aid to Iraq.

1982: Crash of the Souk al-Manakh, an unofficial Kuwait stock market.

CHRONOLOGY

1983: Iranian navy attacks commercial shipping sailing under the Kuwait flag while Iranian-backed terrorists bomb American and French embassies in Kuwait.

1987: Kuwait oil tankers re-flagged as American vessels, giving them protection of the U.S. Navy.

1988: Iran-Iraq War ends in a stalemate but bankrupts Iraq; dictator Saddam Hussein presses the gulf states, particularly Kuwait, for economic assistance.

1990: Iraq invades and occupies Kuwait in August.

1991: An international coalition organized by the United States begins air strikes on Iraq. Operation Desert Storm liberates Kuwait.

1999: Emir Jabir issues a decree giving women in Kuwait the right to vote, but a year later the National Assembly rejects the decree.

2002: Iraq recognizes Kuwait as an independent state and agrees not to attack again.

2003: Arab League holds summit in Bahrain.

GLOSSARY

annex—to take over a territory and incorporate it into another country or state.

assets—in business, tangible items and other resources that can be converted into cash. Assets can include buildings and real estate, stock in corporations and mineral deposits, including oil reserves.

atheism—belief that there is no God.

autonomous—politically independent.

Bedouin—nomadic Arab who travels and trades in the desert.

caliph—spiritual leader in Islam claiming succession from the Prophet Muhammad.

cartel—a political alliance, or alliance of business companies, formed to control production, competition, and prices of a resource.

coalition—a temporary union between multiple groups or nations that agree to work together for a common purpose.

commodity—goods whose future prices are determined by traders on the open market. In addition to oil, commodities include sugar, coffee, oranges and similar foods, as well as precious metals such as gold and silver.

coup—sudden action to overthrow a government, usually by violent means.

desalinization—the process of removing salt from seawater to produce drinking water.

emir—an Arab prince.

emirate—office of the emir; also, the country ruled by an emir.

Islam—the religion of the Muslims, which teaches that Allah is God and Muhammad is his prophet.

Islamist—espousing radically fundamentalist Islamic doctrine that is usually hostile to Western societies and ideas.

mosque—a place of public worship for Muslims.

Muslim—a member of the Islamic faith.

nationalize—to transfer a business, property, or industry from private ownership to government control.

Ottomans—rulers of a Turkish empire that existed from the 1300s to 1919.

GLOSSARY

parliament—a nation's legislative body, made up of elected or non-elected representatives.

petroleum—crude oil that can be refined into gasoline, kerosene and similar substances as well as used in the foundation of plastics.

prophet—a person who speaks for God.

quota—a proportional part or share assigned to each member of a body or organization.

Qur'an—the holy book of Islamic faith, regarded by Muslims as the foundation of their religion, law, and culture. Also spelled Koran.

recession—in economics, the period in which business activity is slowest.

sheik—Arabic ruler, often the head of a family or tribe.

subsidize—to help or promote with public funds.

suffrage—the right to vote.

Torrid Zone—the region of the earth that lies between the Tropic of Cancer and the Tropic of Capricorn.

FURTHER READING

Abu-Hakima, Ahmad Mustafa. *The Modern History of Kuwait*. London: Luzac and Company, 1983.

Al-Mughni, Haya. *Women in Kuwait: The Politics of Gender*. Kuwait City: al-Saqi, 2001.

Al Rashoud, Claudia Farkas. *Kuwait Kaleidoscope*. Kuwait City: The Kuwait Bookshops Co. Ltd., 1995.

Bibby, Geoffrey. *Looking for Dilmun*. New York: Knopf, 1970.

Field, Michael. *Inside the Arab World*. Cambridge, Mass.: Harvard University Press, 1994.

Hilsman, Roger. *George Bush vs. Saddam Hussein: Military Success! Political Failure?* Novato, Calif.: Lyford Books, 1992.

Lawrence, T.S. *Seven Pillars of Wisdom*. New York: Penguin Books, 1979.

Kelly, Michael. *Martyrs' Day, Chronicle of a Small War*. New York: Random House, 1993.

Mansfield, Peter. *The New Arabians*. Chicago: J.G. Ferguson Publishing Company, 1981.

Metz, Helen Chapin, editor. *Persian Gulf States*. Washington, D.C.: Library of Congress, 1994.

Miller, Judith. *God Has Ninety-Nine Names: Reporting from a Militant Middle East*. New York: Touchstone, 1996.

Record, Jeffrey. *Hollow Victory: A Contrary View of the Gulf War*. McLean, Va.: Brassey's US Inc., 1993.

Sasson, Jean P. *The Rape of Kuwait*. New York: Knightsbridge Publishing, 1991.

Viorst, Milton. *Sandcastles: The Arabs in Search of the Modern World*. New York: Alfred A. Knopf, 1994.

INTERNET RESOURCES

http://www.kuwait-info.org

Official Internet site of the government of Kuwait, providing extensive information on many aspects of life in the gulf state. In addition to statistics, visitors can learn about shopping in stores, taking buses, eating at restaurants, and many other aspects of Kuwait's society.

http://www.crsk.org

The web site of the Center for Research and Studies on Kuwait, an institute that examines Kuwait's history and its relations with other countries. The institute has studied social, economic, and political issues faced by Kuwait over the years. The web site includes many historical records about Kuwait, as well as several documents chronicling Kuwait's differences with Iraq.

http://www.opec.org

Official information made available by the Organization of Petroleum Exporting Countries (OPEC), including the history of the cartel and how its members control the worldwide cost of gasoline.

http://memory.loc.gov/frd/cs/kuwait

A country study by the Library of Congress on Kuwait, including details on the country's history, economy, social issues, and environment.

http://www.cia.gov/cia/publications/factbook/geos/ku.html

Facts and figures about Kuwait are available at the CIA World Factbook 2002.

http://www.campdoha.de

Web site of Camp Doha, headquarters of the U.S. Army base in Kuwait.

http://www.kuwaittimes.net

An on-line version of the *Kuwait Times*, an independent English-language newspaper published in Kuwait. In addition to features for Americans and other foreigners living in Kuwait who may be hungry for news from home, the web site includes many stories about life in Kuwait, local weather forecasts, Muslim prayer schedules, and analyses of the news by Kuwaiti commentators.

INDEX

Numbers in **bold italic** refer to captions.

INDEX

INDEX

PICTURE CREDITS

CONTRIBUTORS

The **FOREIGN POLICY RESEARCH INSTITUTE (FPRI)** served as editorial consultants for the MODERN MIDDLE EAST NATIONS series. FPRI is one of the nation's oldest "think tanks." The Institute's Middle East Program focuses on Gulf security, monitors the Arab-Israeli peace process, and sponsors an annual conference for teachers on the Middle East, plus periodic briefings on key developments in the region.

Among the FPRI's trustees is a former Secretary of State and a former Secretary of the Navy (and among the FPRI's former trustees and interns, two current Undersecretaries of Defense), not to mention two university presidents emeritus, a foundation president, and several active or retired corporate CEOs.

The scholars of FPRI include a former aide to three U.S. Secretaries of State, a Pulitzer Prize–winning historian, a former president of Swarthmore College and a Bancroft Prize–winning historian, and two former staff members of the National Security Council. And the FPRI counts among its extended network of scholars—especially its Inter-University Study Groups—representatives of diverse disciplines, including political science, history, economics, law, management, religion, sociology, and psychology.

DR. HARVEY SICHERMAN is president and director of the Foreign Policy Research Institute in Philadelphia, Pennsylvania. He has extensive experience in writing, research, and analysis of U.S. foreign and national security policy, both in government and out. He served as Special Assistant to Secretary of State Alexander M. Haig Jr. and as a member of the Policy Planning Staff of Secretary of State James A. Baker III. Dr. Sicherman was also a consultant to Secretary of the Navy John F. Lehman Jr. (1982–1987) and Secretary of State George Shultz (1988).

A graduate of the University of Scranton (B.S., History, 1966), Dr. Sicherman earned his Ph.D. at the University of Pennsylvania (Political Science, 1971), where he received a Salvatori Fellowship. He is author or editor of numerous books and articles, including *America the Vulnerable: Our Military Problems and How to Fix Them* (FPRI, 2002) and *Palestinian Autonomy, Self-Government and Peace* (Westview Press, 1993). He edits *Peacefacts*, an FPRI bulletin that monitors the Arab-Israeli peace process.

HAL MARCOVITZ is a journalist for *The Morning Call*, a newspaper based in Allentown, Pennsylvania. He has also written about Yemen for the MODERN MIDDLE EAST NATIONS series. He lives in Chalfont, Pennsylvania, with his wife, Gail, and daughters, Ashley and Michelle.